Adobe Photoshop Lightroom Classic 2025 Handbook

The Comprehensive Step-by-step Guide to Advanced Techniques, Seamless Workflow, and Photo Editing for Beginners and Experts

Torren Mercy

CHAPTER ONE
OVERVIEW OF LIGHTROOM CLASSIC

What is Lightroom Classic?

The official product of Adobe, Adobe Lightroom Classic is an advanced photo and video editing program that was specially created for PCs for the convenience of its users. It is well-known for its top features, which enable users to edit, modify, and organize images in a way that makes them look better and cooler. Users of Adobe Lightroom Classic can generate stunning bespoke photos and use them on websites. These images can be saved in a variety of image formats, including JPG, PNG, JPEG, and GIF. All the features you need to transform simple photos into more professional-looking ones, from basic to complex photo or video editing tools, are included in Adobe Lightroom Classic.

The most recent version of Lightroom Classic: What's New?

The most recent version of Adobe Lightroom Classic, version 7.3, includes performance enhancements and feature optimization. Along with batch operation, batch editing, and many other features, lens blur, subject detection, and client presets are ungraded.

- **Correct:** Eliminate the subject background more precisely.

Lightroom Classic's features

The Lightroom Classic App was created especially for laptops. You can use its Premium Features for free to transform your boring photos into vibrant, amazing designs. You can also use it to manage photos or movies on your desktop or laptop computer and save time thanks to its user-friendly interface and quick speed. **The Adobe Lightroom Classic App has the following features, which are covered below:**

- **More Advanced Control Tool:** You now have access to a more sophisticated masking tool that makes it easier and more accurate to choose the picture's editing region.

- **Making a Blur Background:** Simply choose an object or blemish tool in the Adobe Lightroom Classic software, and within two seconds, without choosing a region, the Adobe Lightroom app will automatically choose the image's background and eliminate it.

- **Applying Presets:** You may now utilize Adobe Lightroom Classic's Presets Applying feature, which allows you to apply presets to a certain area of an image by selecting the adaptable presets option.

- **Text** ✏ : You may add text to photographs in a variety of fonts and sizes, as well as colors, shapes, and other elements.

- **Personalized Color** 🖌 : You can apply various hues to your photos in various ways, as well as to the various sections of your images.

- **Cropping** ⌗ : You can utilize several brush types to alter your photos, as well as crop, edit, rotate, and flip them with this app.
- **Fixing Tools** ☑: To improve the image's smoothness and color, you can apply several correction tools in the Adobe Lightroom Classic application.
- **Photographs Gallery** 🖼 : you can create an image gallery there to correctly arrange and utilize the photographs at a later time.
- **User-friendly interface** ▤: Adobe Lightroom Classic has an extremely user-friendly interface that makes it easy for users to locate and utilize the capabilities.

How does Lightroom differ from Lightroom Classic?

- **Adobe Lightroom:** This official Adobe product, the Lightroom app, was created especially for mobile users so they could edit images and movies with their iPhone or Android phone. The Lightroom app can also be used on your iPhone, iPad, Mac, PC, or tablet.
- **Adobe Lightroom Classic:** Designed specifically for desktop users, Adobe Lightroom Classic is an official product of Adobe. Because of the high demand from users, Adobe decided to create the Lightroom Classic app for desktop users, allowing them to enjoy Lightroom's features for free on their desktops.

Features	Adobe Lightroom Classic	Adobe Lightroom
Compatible Devices	only Desktop	Desktop + Mobile + WEB
Location of Content to be Saved	Cloud + Mobile Storage	Cloud + Hard Drive + external Storage Devices
File Backup	No Auto Backup Support	No Auto Backup Support Automatic Backup in Cloud
Recommended for	Only for Professional photographer	Recommended for everyone
Finding photos and organization	Manual keywords Searching	Automatic tagging and intelligence search

Adobe Lightroom Classic's Minimum System Requirements

- **Operating System:** Windows XP, Vista, 7/8/8.1/10

- **Hard Drive Size (ROM):** 2 GB
- **Processor:** intel Dual Core or Higher for best Performance
- **RAM:** 4 GB

Recommended Adobe Lightroom Classic System Requirements

- **Operating System:** Windows XP, Vista, 7/8/8.1/10
- **Hard Drive Size (ROM):** 4 GB
- **Processor:** Core i3 or Higher for best Performance
- **RAM:** 16 GB
- **Graphic Card:** Invidia 4GB

Adobe Lightroom Classic 2025 Overview

A powerful and comprehensive tool for managing and modifying images is Adobe Lightroom Classic. It was designed for photographers who require a methodical approach to handling large quantities of images. Lightroom Classic is designed for desktop usage and has many capabilities for organizing, editing, and exporting photos with complete file management control, in contrast to its cloud-based version, Adobe Lightroom. Lightroom Classic is fundamentally a catalog-based system that allows users to add and save images without altering the originals. In this non-destructive process, each edit, modification, and update to the metadata is preserved independently. This preserves the integrity of the original images. The Library module is a central location where you may arrange your photos. Large photo libraries can be handled more easily with its capabilities, which include keyword tagging, metadata editing, collections, and rating systems. The majority of Lightroom Classic's editing capabilities are found in the Develop module. It offers a vast array of photo-editing capabilities.

Users can adjust exposure, brightness, highlights, shadows, white balance, and colors with extreme precision. You have more control over how a photo appears with more sophisticated features including tone curves, HSL changes, split tones, and color grading. Automated sky and topic selecting, content-aware removal, masking, and other AI-powered features greatly expedite the editing process and ensure superior outcomes. Photographers can use Lightroom Classic's many local modification tools, including the brush tool, graded and radial filters, and AI-powered masking, to enhance particular areas of an image. These features allow users to make selective adjustments, which makes it simpler to highlight specific regions of an image, ensure that exposure is uniform across the image, or creatively alter an image's composition. Additionally, the program's robust batch processing and preset features enable users to edit several photos consistently. Custom presets make it simple and quick to make common modifications and post-processing workflows are made more efficient by allowing edits to be synchronized across a collection of images. In order to achieve specific effects, Lightroom Classic also offers profile-based editing, which modifies colors and tones according to camera profiles.

For photographers working with high-resolution images, Lightroom Classic offers sophisticated capabilities to enhance image quality by lowering noise, sharpening, and resolving lens-related problems. The latest models significantly increase the clarity of images captured in low light with to AI-based noise reduction technologies. With the software's integrated HDR merging and panorama stitching, users may create wide-angle landscapes and high dynamic range photos without the need for additional applications. With Lightroom Classic, users can easily export photographs by modifying output parameters including resolution, file format, compression, and metadata inclusion. This software makes it easy for photographers to showcase their work online by allowing users to post directly to several platforms, including Flickr, SmugMug, and Adobe Portfolio. For those who wish to create authentic prints or photo books that appear to have been professionally created, Lightroom Classic also has modules for printing and book creation. With frequent updates, Adobe continues to improve Lightroom Classic, introducing features that increase speed, include AI-powered tools, and support a wider range of camera models and file types. For photographers who require a high-quality photo editor that allows them complete control over their workflow, from organizing photos to exporting them at the end, it remains the greatest option.

Lightroom Classic 2025's New Features

- **Generative Remove with Detect Objects:** One of the most noteworthy new features is the Generative Remove function, which is powered by Adobe's Firefly AI. Even photographs with complex backgrounds can easily have undesired portions removed with this program. When you simply brush over an object, the Detect Objects tool intelligently locates and selects the entire object, ensuring smooth and accurate removal. This can significantly reduce the amount of time and effort typically required for such jobs.
- **Content Credentials for Digital Asset Security:** To increase the authenticity and security of digital assets, Lightroom Classic 2025 incorporates Content Credentials. Verifiable metadata, like digital signatures and editing histories, are added to an image when you export it using this function. Photographers can now openly discuss the editing process and ensure the integrity of their work for professional and commercial purposes.
- **Improved Denoise for Linear Raw DNGs:** The Denoise feature can now be used with a wider range of file types, including linear DNGs (such as HDR and panorama DNG photos created in Lightroom and Camera Raw), Bayer and X-Trans mosaic raw files, and several proprietary formats from well-known camera manufacturers. Photographers may now capture crisper, more detailed images in a range of shooting scenarios thanks to this advancement.
- **Better Tethering Support with Nikon:** Lightroom Classic 2025 has improved tethering support for Nikon cameras, including the Zfc, Z9, and Z6 III, for studio and tethered shooting scenarios. By eliminating the need for Rosetta Emulation, tethering becomes more responsive and stable, allowing photographers to take and analyze photos faster.

- **HDR Enhancement Adaptive Profiles:** These profiles instantly alter the colors and tones of images to provide a better, yet realistic, starting point for additional editing. Unlike traditional presets, these profiles employ AI to evaluate each image independently and make minor tweaks that enhance the image's visual appeal without sacrificing its natural appearance. This feature is particularly useful for HDR photographs, providing photographers with a powerful tool to get the desired effect with minimal effort.

- **Performance Gains:** Performance has significantly improved, particularly for jobs requiring interactive file editing. When users are masking, adjusting crop angles, and adjusting white balance settings, the brush tool will respond more quickly. Even when dealing with high-resolution images or making intricate adjustments, these enhancements make editing simpler and quicker.
- **Focus Point Selection for Tether Enhancement:** For Sony, Canon, and Nikon cameras, Lightroom Classic 2025 now allow you to select the focus point from within the linked live view window. During tethered shots, photographers can click anywhere on the live view display to set focus areas. Studio photographers who need exact control over focus may particularly benefit from this upgrade.

8. Catalog Backup Management: Managing catalog copies are made simpler by the new backup panel, which is located under Catalog Settings > Backup. Users may quickly access backup locations, view the size of backups, and delete older backups when they're no longer needed. In addition to keeping your workspace tidy and orderly, this feature protects your vital data without using up additional disk space.

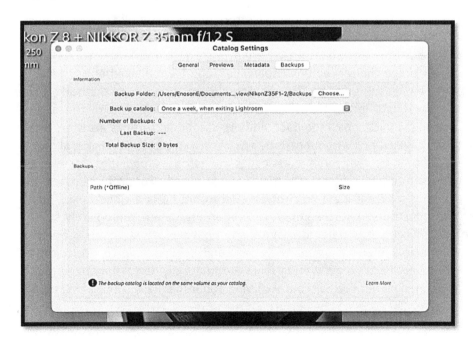

- **Dual Monitor functionality:** With the advent of dual monitor functionality, users may now spread their desktops across two displays. This is useful for handling large catalogs, comparing adjacent images, or designating one screen for the Develop module while the Library module remains open on the other. People are more productive and the editing process is sped up with this kind of independence.
- **Improved Sharing Experiences:** Sharing photos has been more efficient thanks to quicker link creation, more understandable copy and share options, and real-time modification previews. These modifications have made it simpler for photographers to showcase their work to customers, colleagues, or on social media, which expands their following and level of engagement.
- **AI-Powered Innovations:** Lightroom Classic 2025 has several AI-powered capabilities designed to speed up routine editing tasks. Photographers can now enhance their images more accurately and easily thanks to features like Distraction Removal, which can intelligently detect and eliminate photobombers and other undesired objects.
- **Updates to Pricing and Subscriptions:** Adobe has modified their photography plans to demonstrate how its product is constantly improving and becoming more valued. The monthly charge for the Photography Plan (20GB) pre-paid yearly plan has been adjusted to $14.99/month with an annual commitment, although the annual plan still costs $119.88. Users are encouraged to evaluate these changes to determine which plan best fits their needs.

Key Differences between Lightroom Classic and Lightroom CC

Adobe Lightroom comes in two versions: Lightroom Classic and Lightroom CC, which is often commonly referred to as Adobe Lightroom. Both applications are effective tools for photographers, but they work best for different users and in different ways. What sets them apart are their storage choices, editing capabilities, and file management system. The desktop program Lightroom Classic is designed for photographers who prefer a methodical approach and wish to save their data locally. Because it employs a catalog system, the original files are preserved but all modifications, metadata, and organizational settings are stored in a database. This allows for image editing without causing any harm to the original image, allowing for a wide range of modifications. Lightroom Classic has numerous capabilities for file organization, including metadata editing, folders, collections, and keywords. For professionals who deal with a lot of images, this makes it ideal. In contrast, Lightroom CC is a cloud-based application that facilitates and modernizes photo editing. All of your images are immediately saved in Adobe's cloud storage, making it simple to view them on your phone, tablet, or computer. For photographers who prefer having many options and being simple to use, Lightroom CC is a fantastic alternative. Because everything syncs automatically, users may begin working on one device and continue on another without worrying about manually transferring data. Two of the most significant distinctions may be performance and speed. Lightroom Classic allows customers to deal with data saved on their own hard drives and provides them more control over hardware acceleration. This speeds up the editing of high-resolution RAW files. However, depending on how quick your connection is and how large your images are, Lightroom CC's usage of cloud synchronization may cause delays. A greater variety of editing options are available in Lightroom Classic. It has more comprehensive local adjustment tools, tone curves, split toning, advanced masking, and HSL changes. Over time, Lightroom CC has gained many of these functions, but it still lacks some of the more intricate options seen in Classic. For example, Lightroom Classic is the greatest option for professional photographers who need to finish their work swiftly because it supports batch processing and plugins better. Another significant distinction is the option to download and print. Using Lightroom Classic's many export options, users can change file formats, resolutions, color profiles, and watermarking. Additionally, it features a Print module that is ideal for photographers who need to create album layouts or high-quality prints. Lightroom CC, on the other hand, is designed primarily for online photo sharing rather than high-quality printing, and it has simpler export settings. For photographers who work on the road and require instant access to their images from any smartphone or tablet, Lightroom CC is a terrific option. For pros that require a more intricate workflow with strong editing capabilities and local file control, Lightroom Classic remains the greatest option. It ultimately boils down to whether the photographer prefers typical power and control on a desktop or freedom in the cloud.

CHAPTER TWO
UNDERSTANDING CONFIGURATIONS AND INSTALLATIONS

System specifications

Although Adobe Lightroom Classic 2025 is a strong tool for managing and editing images, it requires specific software and equipment to function at its peak. If your computer satisfies or surpasses these requirements, dealing with your images will be easier and faster.

Windows Users

You will need a computer with a 64-bit Intel® or AMD CPU that supports SSE 4.2 or later in order to run Lightroom Classic 2025 on a Windows system. For improved speed, the processor should be able to handle sophisticated instruction sets. For compatibility with the newest features and security upgrades, the operating system should be Windows 10 (64-bit) version 22H2 or later. Although 8 GB of RAM is necessary at minimum, 16 GB or more is advised for more taxing tasks or larger files to maintain system performance. For installation, you will require a minimum of 10 GB of free hard drive space; more space will be needed for catalogs and pictures. Although a 1920 x 1080 display or above will offer a better viewing and editing experience, a monitor with at least a 1280 x 768 display resolution is necessary. A GPU with 2 GB of VRAM and support for DirectX 12 is the bare minimum for graphics processing; however, a GPU with 4 GB of VRAM is advised for tasks requiring a lot of processing power or for use with 4K monitors. It is best to have 8 GB of VRAM in order to fully utilize GPU acceleration features. Software activation, subscription validation, and online service access all require an internet connection.

macOS users

To run Lightroom Classic 2025 efficiently, users need have an Apple Silicon processor or a multicore Intel CPU (2 GHz or faster with SSE 4.2 or later). macOS Ventura (version 13.1) or later is required for the app. 8 GB of RAM is required at the very least, and 16 GB or more is advised for processing larger files or more intricate modifications. For installation, you'll need at least 8 GB of free hard drive space, plus extra for your photo collection. It is crucial to remember that Lightroom Classic will not install on portable flash drives or file systems that use case. Although a 1920 x 1080 display or higher is advised for a better user experience, a display with at least 1024 x 768 resolution is necessary. The minimum requirements for graphics are a GPU with Metal capability and 2 GB of GPU memory; for 4K or higher screens, 4 GB of GPU memory is advised. Either 16 GB of shared memory or 8 GB of dedicated GPU memory is optimal for complete GPU acceleration. Software activation, subscription validation, and online service access all require an internet connection.

Installing Lightroom Classic after downloading it

Designed for photographers who prefer working on their computers, Adobe Lightroom Classic is a robust picture editing and management tool. To ensure that Lightroom Classic is downloaded and installed on your computer correctly, there are a few things you need to perform. **Here is a comprehensive guide to assist you with the process:**

- **Check the requirements for the system:** Make sure your machine satisfies the Lightroom Classic hardware requirements before beginning the download. Assuring compatibility will improve the installation process and provide optimal outcomes.
- **Obtain an Adobe Creative Cloud Subscription:** Lightroom Classic can be used if you have an Adobe Creative Cloud membership. One of Adobe's various plans is the Photography Plan, which includes Photoshop and Lightroom Classic. **How to subscribe:**
  - ➢ Go to the website for Adobe Creative Cloud Plans.
  - ➢ Choose a plan that corresponds with your needs.
  - ➢ To create an Adobe ID or sign in if you already have one, follow the instructions.
  - ➢ Enter the required payment information to finish the subscription procedure.
- **Get the Adobe Creative Cloud Desktop app and install it:** The Adobe Creative Cloud PC app is where you manage your Adobe programs and can download, update, and launch them. To get things going:
  - ➢ Go to the page where you can download Adobe Creative Cloud.
  - ➢ To start the download, click the "Download" button.
  - ➢ Open the installer file after the download is finished.
  - ➢ To install the Creative Cloud desktop application on your PC, adhere to the on-screen directions.
- **Using the Creative Cloud Desktop App, install Lightroom Classic:** After setting up the desktop version of Creative Cloud:
  - ➢ Start the desktop version of Creative Cloud.
  - ➢ Enter your Adobe ID information to log in.
  - ➢ Explore the "Apps" area and find "Lightroom Classic."
  - ➢ Next to Lightroom Classic, click the "Install" button.
  - ➢ Automatically, the application will start to download and install.
  - ➢ After installation, Lightroom Classic can be found in the application directory on your computer or opened straight from the Creative Cloud app.
- **Start Lightroom Classic and turn it on:** Following a successful installation:
  - ➢ Lightroom Classic should open.
  - ➢ If prompted, enter your Adobe ID to log in. The program will check the status of your membership and activate it appropriately.
- **Resolving Installation Problems:** Should you encounter any issues during the installation or download process?
  - ➢ Verify the stability of your internet connection.
  - ➢ Try the installation once more after restarting your computer.
  - ➢ For more help, consult Adobe's official troubleshooting guide.

Adobe Lightroom Classic ought to be installed and operational on your computer if you follow these steps. Because the Creative Cloud desktop software manages updates for all Adobe apps and provides you with access to the newest features and enhancements, it is crucial to keep it updated.

Navigating the interface

Adobe Lightroom Classic 2025 also features a comprehensive layout that makes picture editing quick and simple. For both novice and seasoned editors who wish to maximize their output, it is critical to comprehend its layout and features.

Overview of Modules

Each of the distinct modules that make up Lightroom Classic is responsible for a particular aspect of the photography process. These are the primary modules:

+ **Library Module:** Use the Library Module as a starting point for managing and organizing your photo collection. Here, you may create collections, rate images, add images, and utilize keywords. The Library module offers a variety of photo viewing options, such as Grid and Loupe views, which facilitate browsing and selecting images.

+ **Develop Module:** After organizing your images, the Develop module provides you with a collection of tools for editing and enhancing them. The creative editing process, ranging from simple adjustments like exposure and contrast to intricate color grading and retouching, takes place in this module.

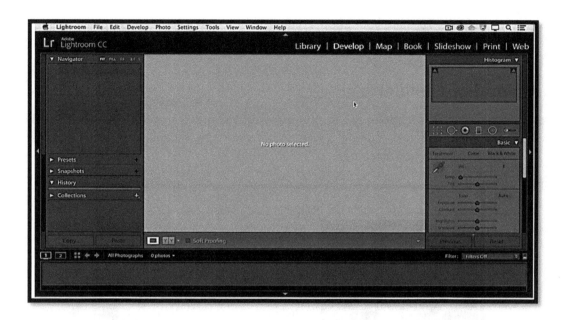

+ **Map Module:** By using GPS data to place your photos on a map, the Map module allows photographers who use geotagging to view the location of each photo.
+ **Book Module:** This module allows you to create picture books. With Lightroom Classic, you can create photo books that appear professional by organizing your images, adding text, and creating layouts.

+ **Slideshow Module:** Create dynamic slideshows of your images that may be utilized as presentations by utilizing unique transitions, music, and themes.
+ **Print Module:** For those who wish to print their images, this module offers a wide range of layout options and print settings to ensure high-quality prints.

- **Web Module:** To share your photos online, create web galleries and upload them. With the help of themes and customization options, this module enables you to create visually appealing galleries.

The layout of the interface

All of Lightroom Classic's modules use the same layout and are designed to be user-friendly:

- **Top Panel:** You may quickly navigate between the modules by using the names displayed on this horizontal bar.

- **Left Panel:** Depending on the module, the left panel may include the Navigator (a preview of the selected image), Presets, Snapshots, and the History of modifications.
- **Right Panel:** This section contains the active module's primary tools and options. The Develop module contains sliders for adjusting exposure, contrast, color balance, and other parameters.
- **Filmstrip:** Located at the bottom, this allows you to swiftly navigate between your photos and select which ones to utilize without ever leaving the current module.
- **Toolbar:** This area, which is situated above the Filmstrip, offers additional tools and viewing choices associated with the module that is now selected.

Comprehending the Catalog System

Users of Lightroom Classic frequently experience problems because they don't completely understand how the Catalog functions or why using different Catalogs is best avoided. The Lightroom Classic Catalog: What is it? Where is it located? How do you support it? We will also discuss the several benefits of using a catalog.

The Lightroom Classic Catalog: What is it?

Your photo information is stored in a SQLite database called the Lightroom Classic Catalog. It contains the metadata for your images as well as all of your developing efforts. The primary database file comes with directories that contain additional data that it requires, like AI masks (used in the Develop module) and previews (used in the Library module). Using a catalog has the advantage of allowing you to alter any type of image file without causing any harm. The most widely used ones, such as Raw, DNG, PSD, TIFF, and JPEG, are included in this. Lightroom is able to accomplish this because it records every modification you make to the Catalog as a set of text commands, or parameters. This is called parametric image editing. Additionally, Develop Presets are parametric. A Develop Preset consists of just a text file with parameters. You can open one in a text editor to read it. **An illustration of some of the text that goes with a Develop Preset is shown here:**

It's simple to see which sliders correspond to which text commands in the Develop module.

What Other Advantages Come with Using a Catalog?

Using a catalog has other advantages:
- **Organization:** To keep your photos in order, you can use Collections, which are robust, adaptable, and effective tools for picture organization. This is not possible with file browsers such as Adobe Bridge.
- You may look for your photos using metadata, including the camera settings, focal length, folder name, and date of capture.
- Your catalog only contains images that you have added yourself. You can't be distracted by the other pictures on your hard disk.
- You can see and edit images without the original files by using Smart Previews. This makes it simple to see and develop images on a different computer or device or while on the go.
- **Lightroom comes in four different versions:** Adobe Portfolio, Lightroom for desktop, Lightroom for mobile, and Lightroom for the web. Synced Collections and Smart Previews allow your Catalog to be in the center.

My Lightroom Classic Catalog: Where Is It?

On both Macs and PCs, the Catalog is initially stored in the Lightroom folder within the Pictures folder. Opening Catalog Settings (Edit > Catalog Settings on a PC or Lightroom > Catalog Settings on a Mac) and selecting the General tab is the fastest way to locate your catalog.

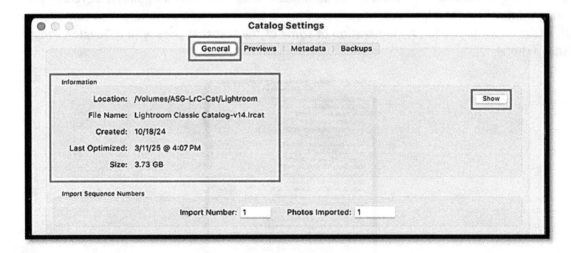

Important information about your catalog, such as its name, location, and size, is contained on this tab. When you select the "Show" option next to "Location," the folder containing your catalog will open in either Windows Explorer (PC) or Finder (Mac). Here is what you will observe:

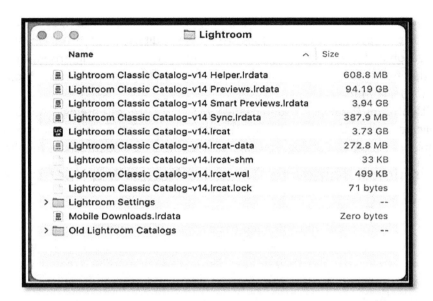

If the names of your catalog and mine differ, so will the names of your files. Each file or folder serves the following purposes:

- Lightroom Classic Catalog-v14 Helper.lrdata: A list of search terms for the folder panel.
- Lightroom Classic Catalog-v14 Previews.lrdata: This file includes thumbnails for standard, 1:1, and minimum previews.
- **Lightroom Classic Catalog-v14 Smart Previews.lrdata:** This file makes up the Smart Preview thumbnails.
- **Lightroom Classic Catalog-v14 Sync.lrdata:** Lightroom Classic uses this cache during syncing.
- **Lightroom Classic Catalog-v14.lrcat:** This is the database that holds details about your images, known as the Lightroom Catalog.
- **Lightroom Classic Catalog-v14.lrcat-data:** Stores masks produced in the Masks window.
- **Lightroom Classic Catalog-v14.lrcat-shm:** When Lightroom Classic is accessed, a temporary folder is created.
- **Lightroom Classic Catalog-v14.lrcat-wal:** When Lightroom Classic is accessed, another temporary folder is created.
- **Lightroom Classic Catalog-v14.lrcat.lock:** This keeps the catalog from being opened by someone else while you are using it. If your hard disk is connected to a network and someone else has access to it, this could occur.
- **Lightroom Parameters:** Lightroom Classic requires a folder containing Develop presets, Export presets, Print module templates, and other files in order to operate correctly. If you have ever used this Catalog box in Preferences > Presets > Location to check the Store presets, it will show up here.
- **Advice:** Don't use this Catalog box to check the Store settings if you're not experienced. It exacerbates problems rather than resolves them.

- **Mobile Downloads.lrdata:** By default, images downloaded from a synchronized phone or tablet is saved in this directory. You can modify the folder in which Lightroom's Synced photographs are stored by selecting Preferences > Lightroom Sync > Specify location for Lightroom's Synced images. I moved the photos to another folder, so they are no longer in this one.
- **Old Lightroom Catalogs:** A folder labeled "Old Lightroom Catalogs" has a compressed duplicate of your Lightroom Classic 13 Catalog. If you have two or more copies of your Lightroom Classic 14 Catalog, you can remove this since you no longer require it.

Three Additional Things to Consider Regarding the Lightroom Classic Catalog

These are the key factors, but you still need to be aware of a few other things.
- **None of your photographs are in the Lightroom Catalog:** Some photographers believe that the Catalog contains their images. Since your picture files are added to the Catalog during the Import process, it is simple to understand why this is believed to be the case. **Let's examine what occurs when you import images into Lightroom.**
  - ➢ When you import photographs, Lightroom adds information about them to the Catalog. This contains the folder in which they were stored as well as any other information, such as camera settings or copyright details.
  - ➢ Lightroom creates previews so you can see the image.
  - ➢ Keep in mind that the Catalog does not save your picture files. The ideal location for them is on a different hard disk.
- **It's best to Use Just One Catalog:** People who used prior versions of Lightroom claimed that adding too many photos to the Catalog would slow things down. Thanks to improvements made by Adobe, you can now add over a million photographs to the Catalog without it becoming sluggish. It makes sense to organize all of your photos using Collections and Collections Sets in a single Catalog. You can only browse and search all of your photographs in this manner since Lightroom can only open and search one Catalog at a time. Other than that, you won't need to backup and monitor multiple catalogs.
- **It's Important to Frequently Backup your Catalog:** Because the Catalog contains so much information about your photographs, frequent backups are necessary to guard against losing the results of all your hard work due to theft or hard disk failure. By default, backups are stored in the Lightroom folder. This is not a good place for it because you will lose both the backup and the catalog if the hard drive fails. The external hard drive contains your Raw files, which is the best place to save the Catalog backup. You must use the use option under Catalog Settings > Backups in order to change the location.

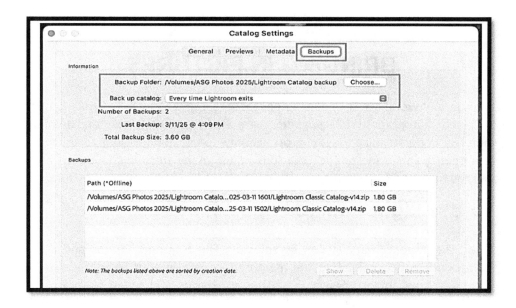

It's also recommended to set up a backup catalog for each time Lightroom exits. For some photographers, leaving Lightroom just once a week is sufficient.

Handling Backups of Lightroom Classic Catalogs

Since the Lightroom Classic 14.2 update, you have control over your catalog backups here. They are listed most recently at the top under backups.

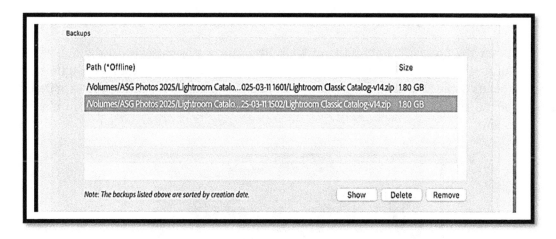

You can use the Delete option to delete a backup from your hard disk by clicking on it. By doing this, you prevent your backups from growing and using valuable hard drive space. Your two most recent backups should be kept. You don't require more than that.

CHAPTER THREE
BRINGING IN PICTURES

A basic step in any workflow is importing photos into Lightroom. Even while it might seem simple to upload photographs into Lightroom, there are important settings and helpful features to be mindful of. Understanding these choices and how to use them to your advantage is helpful to you as a photographer and editor. Let's look at the many steps in the import process and learn about their roles and objectives.

How to Use Lightroom to Import Pictures

- **Open the Import Dialogue Box by selecting File > Import Photos and Video:** Open Lightroom Classic after taking the memory card out of your camera and storing your photos in your folders. Select File > Import Photos and Video from any Lightroom screen. The Import Dialogue Box will open as a result.

- **Open the Source Panel and Find Your Files:** To begin, navigate to the Source panel located on the Import Dialogue Box's left side. You can see your PC's different file folders in the Source panel. Look for your pictures in the folder where you kept them. All of the images will be displayed in the center of the import window when the folder opens.

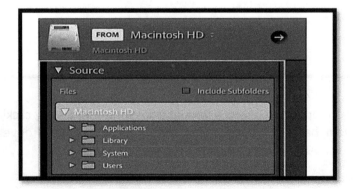

- **Select Your Lightroom Import Method:** What happens when your images are imported depends on each of the four import options.

  - ➤ **Copy as DNG:** This option enables you to simultaneously convert your data to DNG files, move it to a hard disk, and insert your memory card.
  - ➤ **Copy:** This will simultaneously add the images to the Lightroom collection and move them from a memory card to a new spot in your files.
  - ➤ **Move:** When you select this option, the photos will be moved from a memory card to the Lightroom catalog, where they will remain once you're done.
  - ➤ **Add:** This is the best option when importing from a hard drive because it copies the folder and imports it into Lightroom.
- **Click Import after selecting the pictures you wish to import:** The photos you want to upload to Lightroom are now available for selection. A checkmark will appear in the box on the upper left corner of selected photographs, which will turn a lighter shade of grey. To confirm all selected photos and upload several images at once, click the box in the upper left corner of one of the images while holding down the Control (Windows) or Command (Mac) keys. You can also select every photo at once by ticking the box next to All Photos. Every folder photo is selected using this option.

Keep in mind that you cannot import an image if it is grayed out and you are unable to click on it. This usually happens when the file type is prohibited or the image has already been loaded into Lightroom. Now you can click the Import button in the window's lower right corner. Your Lightroom Library will display your photos.

Lightroom's Additional Import Settings Explained

The Panel for File Handling

You can select how Lightroom should display your photo previews using the Build Previews option. Minimal will result in the fastest import because Lightroom just requires a few resources to generate the previews. Embedded & Sidecar will be even faster, even though the previews can be of low quality. Standard will generate a standard preview, whereas 1:1 will provide full-size previews, which will take a little longer. You may also select the best settings for your images with Build Smart Previews. To have Lightroom ignore images that are already in its collection, check the box next to Don't Import Suspected Duplicates. If you would like another copy of your files anywhere in your files, check the box next to Make a Second Copy To and select the location. Finally, if you want to add the file to a specific collection, you can select Add to Collection.

The Panel for File Renaming

As the name suggests, you can rename files using this panel. Renaming them when importing is recommended as you will probably find it simpler to discover the photographs in your Library. Choose one of Lightroom's renaming templates by checking the Rename Files box.

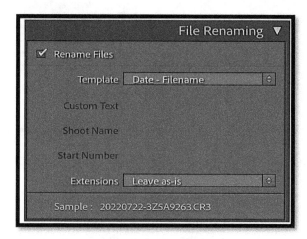

The Panel for Apply during Import

When you import your photos, you can make adjustments and settings in this window. You can make changes later, but they will arrive at the Library already modified. You can use a set of pre-defined Develop Settings by selecting any presets you may have created by clicking the drop-down menu. You can select any predefined metadata you've stored to add to your photos using the Metadata drop-down box. Using keywords enables you to add terms that will help you find your library photographs.

The Panel for Destination

Since you must select where the duplicate image will be stored in your files, the destination panel will only show up if you are importing using the Copy as DNG, Copy, or Move settings. Once the images are in the folder, you can also decide what date format to use and how to arrange them.

How Should You Respond to Greyed-Out Photos?

You may not be able to import or even click on an image that is grayed out. This suggests that Lightroom either does not support the file or that Lightroom has already imported the image. You may quickly resolve this by going to the File Handling tab and unchecking the Don't Import Suspected Duplicates box.

How to Quickly Import Images into Lightroom Classic

I'm always looking for ways to make my Lightroom Classic workflow more efficient. I would like to demonstrate my most recent import procedure to you today. It allows me to swiftly import photos, and it might be helpful to you as well. The trick to importing your photos into Lightroom Classic is to use Sidecar & Embedded Previews. There are a few things you need to do to make it work, and it won't be the best procedure for everyone. I'll examine the options here so you can decide if it would work for you and know what is needed.

Embedded & Sidecar Preview: What Is It?

When you use your camera's Raw format, an additional JPEG is added to the Raw file. Using the integrated JPEG, your camera displays the image on your LCD screen or an electronic viewfinder. Lightroom Classic may also display your photos using the embedded JPEG file in the Library module. This could save you time when importing photos because Standard or 1:1 Previews don't need to be made. I know that full-size JPEGs with the same resolution as the shot are saved in the Raw file by digital SLRs, while smaller JPEGs with lower quality are saved by mirrorless cameras (at least that's what my Fujifilm cameras do). The good news is that if your camera produces low-resolution JPEGs, you can compensate by shooting Raw+JPEG. Even while Lightroom Classic utilizes more hard drive and memory card space, it may still use the JPEG (a sidecar file) for previews. Using the larger JPEG, you may zoom in to check focus and other little elements. I must admit that even though I've been aware of this for a while, I hadn't tried it since I assumed Lightroom Classic would start generating the missing Standard Previews on its own, which would cause a delay. However, I've since discovered a way to use the sidecar or embedded data without requesting that Lightroom Classic create larger previews. This is the procedure.

How to Quickly Import Pictures

First, you need to modify two important Preferences settings.

- Under Preferences > General, uncheck Replace embedded previews with regular previews during idle time.

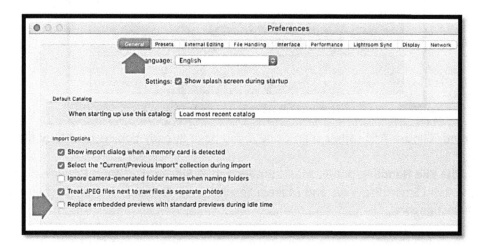

- Next, under Preferences > Performance, select Use Smart Previews rather than Originals for image editing.

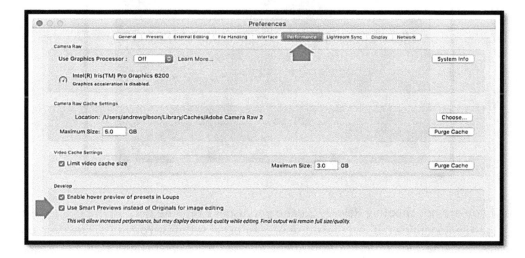

Because they make this process possible, these preferences options are important. This is what you should do the next time you import a group of photos.

a) Verify the photos you want to import into Lightroom Classic's Catalog by opening the Import window.

b) When importing images from a memory card, choose Copy instead than Copy as DNG. There are benefits to switching to DNG, especially if you need to create 1:1 previews. However, I'll explain how to use the Develop module without 1:1 Previews in a moment.

Keep in mind: Choose Add rather than Copy if you have already copied your Raw files to your hard drive.

c) **In the File Handling panel, select Embedded & Sidecar for Build Previews:** Make sure the Build Smart Previews and Make a Second Copy To boxes are left unchecked for the fastest import.

d) If you are not shooting Raw+JPEG and you usually rename files on import, please go to the File Renaming tab and make use of your usual settings. You must, however, uncheck the Rename files option if you shoot in Raw+JPEG. Every imported file is gradually

26

renamed by Lightroom Classic; for example, DSCF0001.jpg and DSCF0001.raf, as my Fujifilm camera would call them, become yourname-01.jpg and yourname-02.raf. The final variable number separates the JPEG from the Raw file; Lightroom Classic does not know where to locate the sidecar profile.

e) In the Apply during Import window, set the Develop Settings to None. Lightroom Classic may create new previews if the Develop parameters are changed, which would delay the import process. Applying a metadata preset (i.e., adding copyright information to the metadata) is possible if you utilize one.

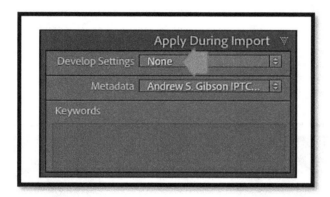

a) In the Destination panel, choose the folder where you want to store your Raw files.
b) Click the Import button to start the import.

Advice: To avoid having to enter these parameters again if you change the settings, you can save them as a quick import preset. Navigate to the Import Preset bar at the bottom of the Import window, select Save Current Settings as New Preset from the drop-down box on the right (it will either display the name of the preset you are now using or state 'None' if you are not using a preset). Give the preset a name, such as "rapid preset." Now, you may set it up here whenever you like.

One thing to note is that in order to ensure that your raw data is moved to the correct location, you will need to change the destination folder each time you perform a new import.

27

How to Edit (Cull) Your Photo Files

This approach works well since the Library module's inbuilt sidecar previews allow you to examine photos. Lightroom Classic can use the embedded/sidecar preview to display the photo as long as you don't alter any Develop module settings. Selecting the photos you want to develop and add to a new collection is the next step. Once you've prepped your photos for development and created a Collection, choose every image in it and go to Library > Previews > Build Smart Previews. You can avoid creating an excessively large Smart Previews file on your hard drive and save time by building Smart Previews for specific files.

The last phase

After selecting a shot, select the 50% zoom option (shown below) in the Develop module's Navigator panel, which is located at the top of the left-hand panels.

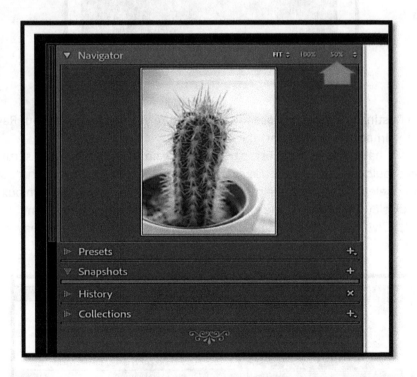

Lightroom Classic zooms into your photo using the Smart Preview. The picture zooms out to Fit view when you click on it again, and it returns to 50% when you click on it again. By doing this, Lightroom Classic is stopped from creating 1:1 Previews, avoiding any delays. This works well for me because I only need a 50% view to process the majority of my photos. If you need a 100% zoom view, choose the photos again and go to Library > Previews > Build 1:1 Previews. By doing this first, the Develop module won't experience any delays.

28

Trade-offs Associated with This Import Process

I'll wrap off with summarizing the trade-offs necessary to make this method work because that's a lot to comprehend.

- Use the Make a Second Copy option to move your data to a backup device or forego converting your photos to DNG if you want to import your files as quickly as possible. Although importing will be slower, you are free to do these things if you so choose.
- If your mirrorless camera has little JPEG previews in Raw files, you must shoot Raw+JPEG. This will give you a full-size embedded profile; the JPEG is the sidecar file.
- Raw+JPEG files cannot be renamed during import since Lightroom Classic renames them gradually. Raw files and JPEG files get disconnected.
- To stop Lightroom Classic from automatically creating 1:1 previews, set the Develop module's zoom to 50%. Rather, it uses Smart Previews, which offer the fastest method.
- Don't make any Quick Develop or Develop module adjustments until you decide which photos you want to develop (the keepers). Lightroom Classic generates a new Standard Preview in the Library module when the embedded or sidecar preview is altered, making it erroneous.

Arranging Pictures in Collections and Folders

Organizing Physically Using Folders

The actual configuration of your computer's hard drive is reflected in Lightroom Classic folders. Images that are loaded into Lightroom remain on your storage system in their original locations rather than physically moving into the software. These files are simply arranged by Lightroom using the folder structure you specified. If you want your photographs to stay in the right order after importation into Lightroom, it is best to organize them in a methodical manner. **Using the format year-month-day, like this:**

```
• 2025
    o  2025-03-10_Wedding_Shoot
    o  2025-04-15_Landscape_Photography
    o  2025-06-05_Family_Vacation
```

This method helps you find your photos later since it keeps them in a chronological, logical order. To prevent broken links, you should always move folders within Lightroom from the Library module.

Organizing Virtually with Collections

Collections are not real storage locations on your hard drive like folders are. Instead, they are online communities that enable you to categorize photos without altering their actual locations. Collections are useful for organizing images by subjects, projects, or modifications.

There are numerous types of collections in Lightroom Classic:
- **Standard Collections:** These manually created groups allow you to drag and drop images into a collection. For example, you could assemble the best images from multiple folders into a "Portfolio Favorites" group.
- **Smart Collections:** These collections automatically sort photos based on certain parameters like file types, star ratings, keywords, and camera settings. To locate your best work, you may, for example, create a Smart Collection that gathers all of the five-star images.
- You can combine multiple collections under a single cover by using Collection Sets, which are folders. For example, you may have separate collections for "Paris Trip," "Iceland Landscapes," and "Tokyo Street Photography" inside a "Travel Photography" category.

Establishing Collections

To establish a fresh collection:
- In the Collections panel, click the plus (+) symbol and choose Create Collection.

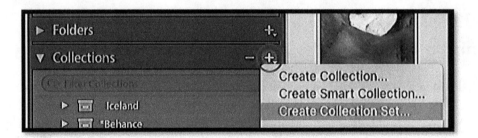

- Press Command + N on a Mac or Control + N on a Windows computer.
- To create a new collection, control-click (Mac) or right-click (Win) on the Collection Set (in the Collections panel) and select Create Collection. Lightroom Classic will select the appropriate Collection Set in the Location field of the Create Collection dialog.

Taking Pictures Out of Collections

The selected photo or photos will be deleted from the Collection but not from the folder or collection if you hit the Delete or Backspace keys while in Grid view.
- Press Cmd + Shift + Option + Return on a Mac. Press Ctrl + Shift + Alt + Backspace on Windows. This will delete an image from a Collection and place it in the Recycle Bin (Windows) or Trash (Mac).
- The current image will be deleted from the Collection but not from the folder or catalog if you hit the Delete or Backspace keys while in Loupe view (in a Collection).
- When in the Loupe view of a collection, pressing Shift + Delete (Mac) or Shift + Backspace (Win) will delete all selected images from the collection, but not from the folder or catalog.

Utilize folders to create collections and collection sets

To create a collection, simply drag a folder from the folder panel to the collections panel. You may either control-click (PC) or right-click (Mac) a folder to create a collection from it.

Using Adobe Cloud to import and sync photos

You can see and edit your photos on a variety of devices, including desktop computers, tablets, and smartphones, when you sync your Lightroom Classic catalog with Adobe Cloud.

- **In Lightroom Classic, enable sync:** Verify that you are logged into your Adobe account. Click the cloud icon in the upper right corner, then select "Start Syncing" to start the sync.
- **To sync, choose collections:** All devices will only be able to view images in synchronized collections. To create a synchronized collection:
  - ➢ To begin, navigate to the Library module and select Collections by clicking the + symbol. After that, choose Create Collection.
  - ➢ Click "Sync with Lightroom" after giving the collection a name.
  - ➢ Include the images you desire in this compilation.
- **Check the Sync Status:** The Cloud symbol indicates the device's level of synchronization. More information about the number of photos awaiting upload or download is displayed when you click on it.
- **View Synced Pictures on Different Devices:** Go to Lightroom Web or download the Lightroom app to your phone. Enter your Adobe ID to view and modify your synchronized collections.

CHAPTER FOUR
ABOUT THE LIBRARY MODULE
An overview of the Library Module

The Library module is one of the two most crucial steps in the Lightroom Classic process. There, you may view, search, sort, and browse your whole collection of images. How is the system configured, then? What are the functions of the tools? How do you obtain the necessary tools? The configuration of the Library module is identical to those of the other Lightroom Classic modules. It features expandable toolbars at the top and bottom, bars for additional controls at the top and bottom, and vertical sidebars on the left and right of the screen. I leave these flat most of the time. All seven of the Lightroom Classic modules are shown in the top toolbar, which you may click to launch. You have the option to leave this open, but it will be displayed momentarily if you move the mouse pointer over the top of the screen. The items from the Folder or Collection you selected in the left sidebar are displayed as a film strip in the bottom toolbar. I conceal the filmstrip because it's not always helpful. In any case, the thumbnail view of the main window displays the same images. Let's get on to the crucial stuff.

View Modes for Library Modules

Simply put, view styles are several methods of displaying your images on the screen for various tasks, such as selecting which images to display.

a) **The E keyboard shortcut for loupe view:** Loupe View displays the image you are working on in the central panel at a time. Use the arrow keys to navigate to the previous or next image, or click on another image in the filmstrip. This will alter the image seen in loupe view. In this perspective, you can also enlarge a picture to examine more of its details. When choosing which shots to refrain from shooting, it's useful to examine how sharp the focus is (if you're as meticulous as I am).

b) **Grid view (G shortcut on the keyboard):** Lightroom's library grid view option allows you to see several images in both the grid and the film strip (more on this later). I primarily utilize Lightroom's Grid and Loupe views. I use grid view to scroll through images in a collection or folder or to swiftly view a large number of images. You can view all the photographs in one easy place. It's also possible to modify the thumbnails' size so that you can see more or less rapidly.

c) **3. Compare View (Shortcut to the C Keyboard):** The "candidate" image on the right and the image you "select" on the left are the two images displayed in the middle panel of Compare view. Once the candidate's photo has been displayed, you can click on another image to view it on the "select" side. Clicking on another image in the filmstrip will cause it to swap places with the image on the side you selected. This view could be helpful to certain persons who wish to compare multiple images. I don't use it myself. I prefer poll perspective.

d) **The N keyboard shortcut for survey view:** When I'm sifting through a collection of comparable photographs, I frequently use poll view to select the best image. I use it a lot when I'm selling anything in person because it also helps the client select their finest photos. In the Survey view, you may select how many images to display in a grid. It resembles a hybrid of compare view and grid view.

e) **View of People (keyboard shortcut O):** I don't utilize People View because I exclusively take portraits and don't need to locate a subject I've photographed numerous times over the years. You might utilize it to snap photos of your loved ones. The good news is that Lightroom provides all the information you require about this view when you click the "People" option in the menu or hit the "O" key in the Library module.

Overview of the Classic Library Module Layout in Lightroom

Similar to the other Lightroom modules, the library module is organized logically. You will often work from top to bottom and left to right on the screen. **Before I go into how to utilize each tool set in the library module, let's take a moment to review the setup.**

a) **The top panel:** The top panel displays the module selection. You can shift from one stage of your process to the next in Lightroom by clicking on the right tab (also called module). Regardless of the module you are in, it remains unchanged. All you need to do is click on the Library tab to return to the Library module after working on images in the Develop module. Pressing the E key on your computer will significantly speed up your work.

b) **The Left Panel**

The Lightroom library module's left panel is used for: Arranging images as you would in a real library; navigating around the active image (the one you now have open); and sending images to your hard drive or other publishing sites (as an alternative to exporting).

  c) **The Right Panel:** Lightroom's right panel is where you access and view information about the current photo.

Where can you find it?

> ➤ To make finding a photo easier, provide keywords. To view your photo's data, including the histogram and metadata, add comments.
>
> ➤ You can also make a basic adjustment to your photo, but I'll go into more depth about that when we examine the right panel.

d) **Tool Bar (T shortcut on the keyboard):** The gray bar behind your primary image or photo grid is called the toolbar. Regardless of the view mode you're in (we'll discuss view modes in more detail shortly), it remains unchanged. If you can't see it, it may be hidden.

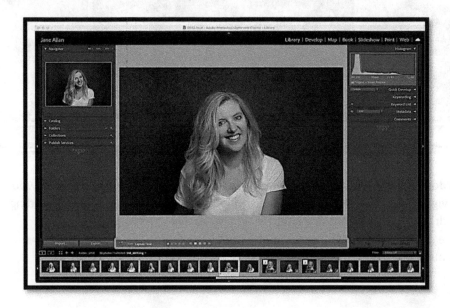

Then either:

- Either press T on your keyboard to use the shortcut key to display it, or choose View in the menu at the top of the screen and then deselect "Hide Toolbar."

You can alter the menu to suit your needs and improve the usability, but it might include buttons for ten jobs in total. Some jobs have many buttons. I believe you should only have the functions you utilize so you don't get too much information.

You may also use the keyboard to press a lot of the buttons. You won't need to press the buttons if you are familiar with these. The size of your screen determines how many features you may access in the toolbar. In other words, all of the toolbar's capabilities won't fit if you have a small screen. My 15-inch MacBook would not display all the features, but my 27-inch iMac will. You may not be able to figure out how to turn something on or off if you don't keep this in mind. **The following are some toolbar functions:**

- View Modes
- Sorting
- Flagging
- Rating
- Color label
- Rotate
- Navigate
- Slideshow
- Zoom
- Draw Face Region
- Grid Overlay

The loupe view image is located at the top of the menu, while the grid view with the additional thumbnail slider is located at the bottom.

Additionally, grid view offers the ability to add:
- A painter
- The size of the thumbnail

Out of the three functionalities in my toolbar, I only show two:
- Sorting
- Rating
- The size of the thumbnail

I don't utilize Draw Face Region or Grid Overlay, and the other tools offer far more user-friendly computer shortcuts.

How to configure the toolbar

- To the right of the menu, you must click on the upside-down triangle.
- A drop-down menu will show up. It will display the items in your toolbar that are checked.

- To select or reject a feature, click on it.
- e) **The film strip:** The toolbar is above the picture clip film strip. As it sounds, it appears like a film strip. Above it is a black bar of icons. Here, every image in a certain folder or collection is displayed in a lengthy row. To display an image or collection of images in the middle panel, click on the thumbnail of an image or group of images in the film strip. When you select multiple photos in film strip (or grid view, for that matter), the surrounding region appears lighter in color than the other photographs. Even lighter is the picture you're working on or the one that was selected initially.

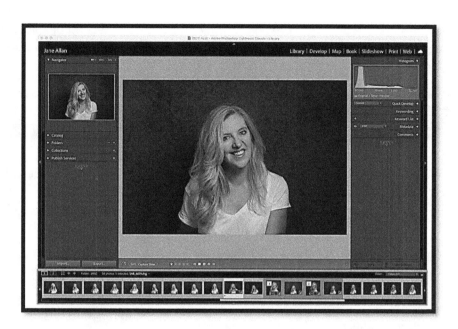

A black bar above the images

Between the toolbar and the images is a black bar with several buttons. Like the menu, this can also be extremely busy and clog your screen. For this reason, I click the word "Filter" to reduce the size of the filter area.

The icons are as follows, going from left to right:
- There are two squares with the numbers 1 and 2. Click 1 to open the main window only, and click 2 to open a second window. I never use this feature.
- 4 block grid — Switches to grid view (I like to hit the special key)
- **Arrows:** I don't see why they are there; they are for traveling to and from the previous view you used (grid, loupe, comparison, survey, etc.), not for switching between photographs. To switch the view mode, utilize fast keys rather than navigating back and forth.
- **Folder (or Collection):** This displays the address of your photo (the folder in which it is located), the number of photos selected, the image file name, and, if it is a virtual copy, the copy number to indicate whether you have created multiple copies. If the image you are working on is in a folder, the text will read Collection rather than Folder. Very beneficial!

- **Filter:** This feature displays icons for filtering images in a collection or folder according to attributes such as color rating or the condition of the folder. It is a photo search engine. To see or conceal the options, click the word "Filter."

I only ever glance at the address feature on this bar. I can easily see the number of selected photos, the folder or collection I'm in, and the title of each image.

The Film Strip's Image Thumbnails

When you modify an image, badges—what Lightroom refers to as icons—appear on picture thumbnails in the film strip. **You may rapidly determine whether a picture has been altered, particularly if it's:**
- Cropped
- Has evolved modifications (i.e., it has been revised)
- Contains GPS coordinates.
- Is part of a collection
- Is in a rapid collection
- A digital replica of an image

Clicking on these icons will have no effect if you haven't unchecked the "Ignore click on badges" box in your Lightroom preferences. They are merely brief guides. But that's not the end of it. **On the film strip, you can easily view images that have:**
- Star ratings
- Labels for colors
- Rejected or flagged

These are all excellent methods for selecting the finest images from a shoot. Instead of using the flag and rejecting OPTION, I prefer to use color designations and star grading.

The Lightroom Library Module's left panel

Recall that I stated that Lightroom is logically organized and that the process proceeds from top to bottom and left to right. We'll start at the top of the left side and work our way down, just like you would when working in Lightroom. As you can see, I also call the tools in the panels on the left and right. The reason they are referred to as "panels within panels" is that each one contains a collection of tools that are helpful for the task at hand. Panels and tools are simply a technique to group jobs; don't get caught up in the details. By clicking on the triangle in the top left corner of each panel, you can open and close all of the panels on the left and right sides of the screen.
   a.   **The Navigator Panel**

The portion that is visible when the image is 50% compressed is shown by the white border surrounding it. Unless you move your cursor over a photo in the film strip, the image you are working on is displayed in the explorer panel. After that, the image beneath your mouse will be displayed. **This is useful but challenging to comprehend:**

- Useful if you want to quickly view a larger version of an image in the filmstrip;
- Perplexing if you forget that your mouse is resting on a filmstrip photo rather than the photo you're working on.

There are four ways to zoom in and out of the image you're working on in the upper right corner of this panel:

- Toggle between Fit and Fill by using the two triangles.
- 100% to enlarge the image by 100%
- The following figure that appears, such as 200%, indicates the latest zoom percentage that was utilized other than 100%.
- Alternatively, to choose another percentage to zoom into, click the two triangles.

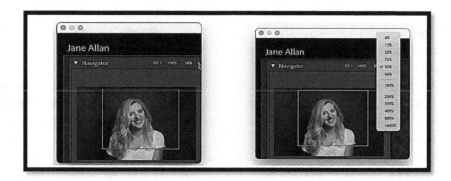

The option that is indicated by white lettering indicates the zoom level you are on. Click on the image once more to zoom in or out. Clicking on a zoom level in the navigator panel while in grid view will immediately zoom in to loupe view.

Click and drag on the browser panel to move around the image while it's zoomed in. In the center of the screen, click and drag the image you wish to modify.

  b. **The catalog panel**

The store panel is quite user-friendly. There are four methods to see the images in your Lightroom Classic album:

  - **All Photographs:** This function displays every image in your Lightroom collection.
  - **All Synced Photos:** This displays every picture you have that is in sync with Lightroom Mobile. Drag photos to this collection to sync them with Lightroom Mobile. To activate sync, however, first click the cloud icon in the top right corner of the screen.
  - **Quick Collection:** Every image you have contributed to a quick collection from one or more folders is in one location. It's quite helpful for assembling images from many eras that are all connected by a common topic. When I'm searching for images for these postings, this is really helpful.
  - **Previous Import:** This displays the images that you recently imported into Lightroom.

c. The folders panel

Lightroom folders follow the same structure as your PC files. Lightroom is where any modifications to this arrangement must be made. For instance, you are unable to create a new folder, change its name, transfer or remove an existing one, or perform any other action. Remember that the (potentially) RAW files you work with in Lightroom Classic are only a preview of the final files you will export from Lightroom in (likely) JPEG format. To keep your photographs organized in Lightroom and on your computer, the folders panel is crucial. Photos and folders may not appear in your library since you probably modified a folder on your computer rather than in Lightroom.

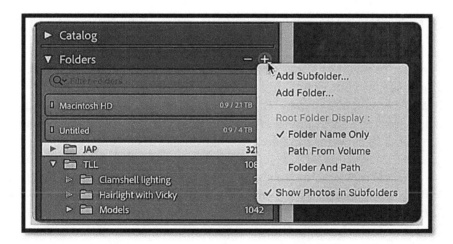

+ Click the + symbol at the top of the folder to create a new one.
+ Click the tiny triangle next to the plus sign to alter the way the folders are displayed. "Folder Name Only" is selected, and "Show Photos in Subfolders" is checked.
+ To view a folder's whole location on your computer, move your cursor over it.
+ Each folder's number on the right indicates the total number of images in that folder and all of its subfolders.

- Subfolders are located in folders with a complete triangle next to the name. Subfolders are absent from folders with faded circles.
- Select a folder and click the minus symbol next to the plus symbol at the top of the folders panel to remove it.

d. **Collections Panel**

Unlike folders, which are fixed filing structures, collections, such as a working folder, are more ephemeral. **There are two kinds of picture groupings in the collections panel:**
- Regular collections made by you;
- Preloaded smart collections made by Lightroom and any you create

I frequently use collections because they allow me to rearrange the arrangement of images inside a collection and move images from various folders into and out of collections. Sets of collections are another option.

I use collections like these when I deal with my photo clients.
- Suppose I take pictures of The Queen.
- I would import the photos into a folder called The Queen, then compile all of the shots from the shoot into a collection called The Queen. Finally, I would select the best ones to show my customer, The Queen.
- I would make a collection set called The Queen Final following the viewing, for which I do employ a star grading method in the Lightroom Library module.
- After that, I would compile the album images into a collection called The Queen album and include them in the collection set.
- The Queen wall is a collection of wall prints that I would use in the same way.
- Using the Queen Final collection set, I would then give the pictures one last polish.
- I would choose every picture in the Queen Album collection and export it using an album print export preset I made.
- I would use an export preset for wall prints to export every image in The Queen wall collection.

e. **The panel for publishing services**

Lightroom Classic has the following marketing websites already configured. You just fill them in with your own details using the pop-up text box.

- A hard drive
- Adobe Stock
- Flickr

Additionally, there is a button that allows you to search for additional online services. Adobe Stock is the only item from the share services panel that I don't utilize. I prefer to use the export menu over the hard drive post service when I want to save images to my hard drive.

f. **Buttons for import and export**

When you launch Lightroom, the library module appears first. You can press the import button to access the import screen immediately if it doesn't appear after inserting the memory card into the card reader. To save the images to your computer for printing or posting online, click the "export" button. To speed up the exporting of several photos, set up export presets.

The Lightroom Library Module's right panel

The library module's right panel is where you may modify and add metadata to your images, enter keywords, and make basic adjustments.

    + **The Histogram Panel**

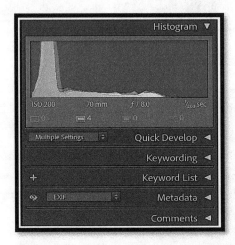

Both the library module and the develop module display the Lightroom graph. In the library module, it serves merely as information, but in the develop module, you may click and drag on it to modify the color in various tonal zones.

    + **The Quick Develop panel**

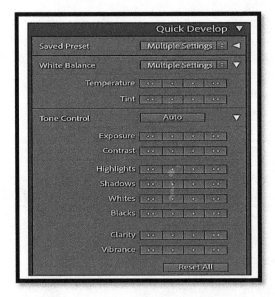

Use Lightroom's rapid develop panel if you need to do some basic tweaking quickly. However, I wouldn't process pictures with it. You have the following options:

➤ Utilize a preset in Lightroom.

➤ You may either select Custom or then adjust the white balance as you wish by clicking on the triangle on the right, or you can select Auto and let Lightroom adjust it for you.

➤ You can use Tone Control to make simple tone adjustments by choosing Auto or by hitting the sideways arrow to see all of your options.

The Develop module's primary interface is quicker and simpler to use. The only time this isn't true is when you wish to utilize a preset on a group of photos. In the library module, select the images you wish to work with. Next, navigate the menu by opening Saved Presets in the rapid develop panel.

➤ **The Keywording Panel**

Using keywords is a helpful strategy when searching through a large catalog for images. Important keywords should be entered into the box, separated by commas, so that they can be used to locate your image. Every shoot is stored in a genre-specific folder, with a subdirectory for every client. Keywording is not a part of my business process. I can add the year and location to the keywords, which makes them helpful for personal photos, particularly those from trips. You may click on the keyword ideas in Lightroom to add them to your existing keywords. You can create your own keyword set or utilize one of the pre-installed Lightroom keyword sets, such as the portrait keyword set.

↓ **The Keyword List panel**

All of the keywords that have been applied to images in the catalog are listed here. It serves as both a search engine and a method of adding keywords to an image. A mark appears on the left and an arrow appears on the right when you move the mouse pointer over a keyword.

➢ To include the keyword in your image, check the box.
➢ To view every image that contains the keyword you moved the cursor over, click the arrow. As you can see, additional keywords that were used in conjunction with this one will also be examined.

↓ **The Metadata Panel**

This displays the camera's metadata, including the lens, focal length, time, date, picture number, and any additional information that was added to the image. If a metadata preset is configured to be utilized during the import process, it will contain contact details and copyright information. **If the appropriate preset is selected, these details will also be displayed here.**

- **Comment Panel:** Pictures sent out through the Publish Services panel fall under this category. The comments displayed are those left on the website where the image was uploaded. They aren't useful for taking notes regarding your photos.
- **Buttons for Sync and Sync Settings**

The Sync button in the Library module is used to match data between various images. The Sync settings button lets you sync the edit settings (i.e., the changes you've made) across different images, much like you would in the Develop module. Sharing settings doesn't need you to enter the Develop module, which saves you time.

To make the workspace simpler and give you more room to work on the image, use a loupe view with the side panels concealed.

Customize the Library Module to Your Needs

Adobe made Lightroom Classic just when you thought they had considered every possibility. Here are some further suggestions for simplifying your life. Since you now have a few additional options to organize your desk, they must have understood how difficult it is to keep track of all these gadgets.

- ⊹ **Parts of the Library module can be hidden or shown.**
  - ➢ To conceal or reveal the left and right panels, use the tab.
  - ➢ To hide or reveal all panels, use Shift + Tab.

Additionally, you can click on the tiny triangle in the center of the panel's edge to reveal or conceal each one individually. On a small screen, this feature lets me free up more space for the running image. It is also applicable to the Develop module. It frees up room, which is why some people prefer it.

Only one tool panel is accessible at a time while the library panel on the left is in solo mode.

- ⊹ **The Solo Mode:** Solo mode is a fantastic method to simplify your Lightroom workspace when it comes to chaos. When solo mode is enabled, only one tool panel will be visible at once. In other words, the Folder panel will automatically close when the Catalog panel opens if you click on Folder and then Catalog. **To activate or deactivate solitary mode:**
  - ➢ Use the right-click menu when you hover over a panel header text, such as Catalog.
  - ➢ From the drop-down menu, choose solo mode.

⁕ **Modify the Panel's Size:** Similar to other Lightroom modules, you may adjust the size of a panel in the Library module by clicking and dragging its edge. To make your thumbnails easier to see, click on the top portion of the filmstrip panel and drag it up. This will enlarge the filmstrip. Small images with bugs? Simply enlarge the filmstrip, and the badges will reappear.

⁕ **Select the Info Overlay Display Method:** You can decide which information layers to display in grid view and loupe view, as well as whether to display any at all. To switch between three options or to reveal or conceal the information display while in Grid view mode, press the shortcut key J. To reveal or conceal the information window or to navigate between two options in Loupe view, press the shortcut key I.

Essential Keyboard Shortcuts for Working in the Library Module

You won't even need to think about it if you use the computer shortcuts, which will help you recall things rapidly.

B: Include in quick collection

E: View of the Library module loupe

G: Grid view of the library module

N: Survey view of the library module

T: Toolbar (on/off switch)

Give the picture a star rating between 1 and 5.

6–0: Give the picture a color label (6 being red, 7 being yellow, 8 being green, 9 being blue, and 0 being purple).

Show/hide side panels tab

To reveal or conceal all panels (top, bottom, and sides), press Shift + tab.

To enable auto-advance after adding to a fast collection, star rating, or adding a color label, use caps lock in combination with B or the number keys.

CHAPTER FIVE
ABOUT THE DEVELOP MODULE

Overview of the Develop Module

Lightroom Classic has distinct modules for organizing and editing photographs. Changes to your images are made in the Develop module. When in the Develop module, Lightroom Classic has two sidebars on the left and right. The top and bottom bars above and below the image you're working on also have additional controls.

A. Presets, Snapshots, History, and Collections panels B. Toolbar C. Histogram D. Photo Information E. Smart Preview Status F. Tool strip G. Adjustment panels

Along the page's edges are a series of tiny "disclosure" lines. To create extra space for your image, you can use them to collapse and conceal the top and bottom bars, as well as the left and right sidebars. The left and right column bars will typically remain open while the top and bottom bars are hidden. A list of all the other Lightroom Classic modules is displayed in the top bar for easy access. In contrast, a slideshow for the selected Folder or Collection is displayed in the bottom bar. When only one image is displayed at a time in Develop mode, this can be useful. However, you may always return to the Library module and select a different image. The Filmstrip bar isn't always quick or simple to use. Personally, I don't utilize it. The major work is done in the left and right sidebars, so let's look at them.

Develop Module Sidebar on the Left

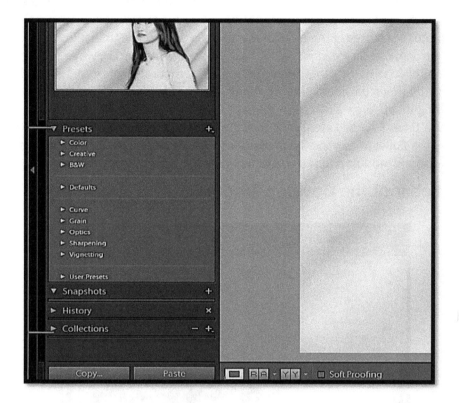

You may quickly add immediate looks using the Presets panel, go back through your changes using the History panel, and take screenshots of editing stages that you may wish to review later in the left sidebar. The History and Snapshots panels are frequently overlooked despite their usefulness. Additionally, the Develop module has a Collections panel, which is the only option to browse among images.

To put it briefly, this is how they operate. The presets panel allows you to apply a predefined set of adjustments to any image. These can offer artistic tone or vignetting effects, as well as alter standard elements like color and exposure. Later iterations of Lightroom can also employ "adaptive presets" to alter specific areas of your images with AI masking. You can undo or modify these defaults at a later time, provided they don't erase anything. Since we are already discussing this type of modification, the History panel is for it. It displays every modification and alteration you have made to your image thus far. Even if you exit Lightroom or switch to a different image, all of this is preserved. To see what you did and what transpired, you can go back and review all of the adjustments you've already made. After you've finished searching, you can both go back to a previous History state and alter the edit's direction, or you can make your most recent modifications once more. That's fantastic. However, what if you could also save specific points in History for easy access? The Snapshots panel is where you may do that. For photographers who wish to edit their images in a systematic and scientific manner, this is fantastic. Although you have a lot of power and control with the History and Snapshot panels, some people, like me, may find them overwhelming. In addition to being useful, the Collections panel provokes thought. How are you going to arrange your photos? Since they make it obvious where the photos are stored, genuine folders make the most sense to many photographers. The folders in Lightroom Classic are identical to those on your computer. However, Lightroom Classic also features Collections. In other apps, these are sometimes referred to as albums. They function similarly to virtual containers, combining images from many directories and locations without altering them. Images can be in as many Collections as you like, but they can only be in one folder at a time. But the key issue is that the Folders panel is not displayed in the Develop module; only the Collections panel is. Unpleasant? The decision is yours. Since it's so simple to return to the Library module and select another folder, it doesn't really matter.

Right Sidebar of the Develop Module

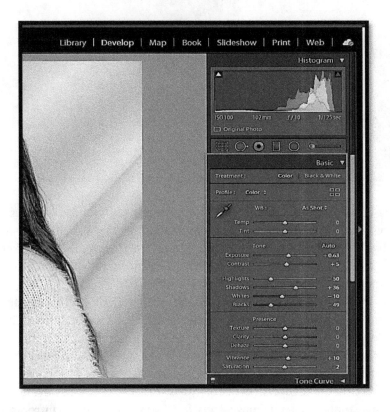

The actual editing takes place here, and it consists of multiple panels. You can utilize the Histogram panel at the top of the screen to see if your modifications are removing the highlights or the shadows from the image. The next item in this section is a tools strip. Edit is the most used option here, followed by Crop, which places a cropping option at the top of the panel list, Healing/Remove, which adds a retouching panel, Red-Eye Correction (who needs red-eye correction anymore?), and Masking, which displays all of Lightroom's regular masking tools and clever AI.

All right, let's discuss the Edit panels. The Basic panel of Lightroom Classic contains some of its most helpful features. It allows you to adjust Adobe's "Presence" settings for Texture, Clarity, and Dehaze as well as White Balance, Exposure, and Contrast to enhance the tones. We'll discuss further in a separate part. The other panels are more specialized, with the exception of the Tone Curve panel. This is equivalent to adjusting the curves in Photoshop or any other image editor. This is helpful for making adjustments to tone and contrast as well as certain color changes within the tonal range of the image. The HSL/Color panel allows you to alter specific colors in an image. Although this can be used for a variety of editing chores, it's particularly helpful for adding analog, vintage, or vintage effects. It's fascinating because clicking the "B&W" button at the top of the column opens a "B&W" panel where you may alter the original image's colors to make them appear more or less grayscale. This more sophisticated approach can be used in place of the outdated Photoshop Channel Mixer method. The Color Grading panel performs two primary functions. It is possible to alter the hue, brightness, and intensity of the highlights, midtones, and shadows in an image. This can be used for split-toning and toning effects in black and white, as well as for some color effects. Noise reduction and enhancement are also possible using the Detail panel. on summary, you can utilize these to achieve the ideal balance between sharpening and lowering noise on an image, albeit they will also have their own pieces. The handy and cool Lightroom Denoise tool is also available here. The Lens Corrections panel will handle itself most of the time. You may need to manually tick the Remove Chromatic Aberration box, but Lightroom Classic will typically discover and use a lens adjustment setting for your camera. This panel also includes a tab named "Manual corrections." The Transform panel is excellent for resolving perspective issues like as lines that join together, as Lightroom might not be able to locate a repair model. Most sorts of photography don't require this, but building photos—especially those where the design is crucial—do. While manual modifications are possible, automatic ones typically function fairly well. You can add a grain effect and a creative vignette effect, which is often more expressive and useful than it seems, using the Effects panel. Those who enjoy vintage analog effects will love Lightroom Classic's grain effect because it's incredibly realistic and easy to manipulate. With the advent of more contemporary features like Profiles, it's time to retire the Calibration panel. This is the place to go if you still want to use outdated techniques that don't exactly fit with the times. That concludes the discussion of the Develop module's right part and the Develop module as a whole. Although this is a brief overview of the Develop module's capabilities, it is a crucial component of Lightroom Classic's editing tools, and in order to get the most out of it, you must understand what it can accomplish.

The Detail Panel: Sharpening

Lightroom has an extremely potent editing tool. It can be found in the "Detail" panel of the Develop module. It functions similarly to Photoshop's "Unsharp Mask" tool, but it's superior because it offers additional options for enhancing your images. Prior to discovering Lightroom, I had to use Photoshop to sharpen each image, which was tedious, time-consuming, and destructive because you couldn't undo the edits you made. Unlike Photoshop, Lightroom does not alter images; instead, depending on the type of file, modifications are saved in the image headers or a separate file. I can use the previous panel to restore the image to its initial condition or reverse any modifications I've made in case I make a mistake or wish to return to the original image. The ability to specify custom parameters for images during the import process is another time-saver, particularly when dealing with hundreds of photos.

Settings for Sharpening

It's always preferable to explain anything with examples. Open a sample image in Lightroom first. Next, take the following action:

- Click "Develop" in the upper right panel or hit the "D" key on your PC to open the Develop module.
- Left-click your photo to see it at 100%. Prior to adjusting the sharpening, I strongly advise you to view your photographs at 100% magnification.
- In Lightroom, open the right panel and go down to "Detail."

The detail panel will appear as follows:

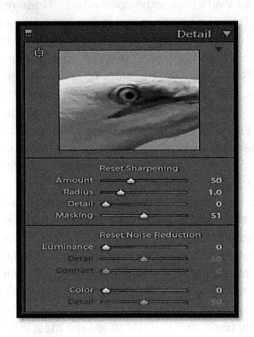

The Sharpening Tool has four different kinds of sliders:

- **Amount:** "Amount" refers to the amount of editing you wish to apply to a photo; zero indicates no sharpening at all. As the number increases, you will notice greater clarity. Additionally, excessive sharpening will increase the loudness. I usually leave the value at 50 for my photos, but occasionally I can change it depending on the image and noise level.
- **Radius:** The size of the cutting area surrounding the edges is expressed in terms of radius. Lightroom will sharpen the borders by greater than one pixel if you leave the setting at 1.0. I usually keep the radius value below 1.5 since if you set it to 3.0, the

sharpening would be dispersed over three pixels around the border, making the lines larger and more "shadowy."

- **Detail:** As the name implies, the "detail" tool allows you to adjust the degree of sharpening applied to the image's edges. Big edges are only sharpened by a low number, such as 0. All edges, no matter how tiny, become sharper when the value is high, such as 100. For instance, just the edges of the thick feathers in a bird image will become sharper if the detail level is left at "0". However, even the tiny feathers will become sharper and stick out if you select a number higher than 50. I make an effort to maintain the detail scale below 50 when I shift it. This is due to the fact that larger numbers typically produce a lot more noise.
- **The most practical and adaptable function is masking.** It conceals sections that don't require improvement, much like Photoshop's mask tool does. Additional noise will be added around your items by adjusting the "Amount" and "Detail" settings. It will be eliminated by this tool. It works best for images where the subject is distinct from the background, but it isn't very helpful for images with a lot of lines or details. It functions best on a soft, blurry background. Check out these examples.

By combining all of these options, you may significantly reduce the amount of time you spend working and enhance your photos with little effort. This actual image can be used to demonstrate how to enhance it in Lightroom.

The Alt/Option Key

To ensure that you wouldn't miss it, this needed its own header. Press the Option key if you're on a Mac. If you're on a computer, hit the Alt key. One of the most difficult aspects of the procedure is observing how sharpening alters your images. While viewing the image at 100% is helpful, Lightroom users frequently become confused when experimenting with features like masking, detail, and radius since minor adjustments may not be apparent while viewing the image. The Alt/Option key is useful in this situation. Press the Option or Alt key on your keyboard. Then, to select one of the four settings, slide the bar from left to right with the mouse. **Here is what you will observe:**

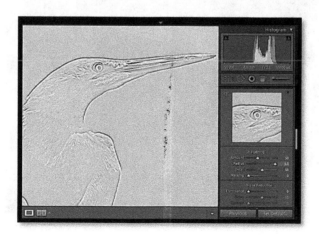

And when I move the "Radius" scale and hit the Alt key, this is how the image appears. I can clearly see how the radius will alter my image thanks to this. At the highest level of "3.0," you can see that the radius around the margins is too thick, giving the image an odd appearance and creating black shadows around the subject. The effects are also visible on a gray background if we shift the Amount and Detail scales while holding down the Control or Alt key. This helps us anticipate how the scene will alter the image. The "Masking" tool's functionality is slightly altered when the Option or Alt key is used. As previously said, the masking tool is used to sharpen only the borders of the image while leaving the smooth areas intact. We can alter the starting point of the lines by moving the slider from 0 to the right. When the value is "0," the entire image is sharpened because no masking is used. Even if there wasn't much noise in the sky to start, sharpening will make it noisier because it's a smooth background. **The following events occur as you move the scale:**

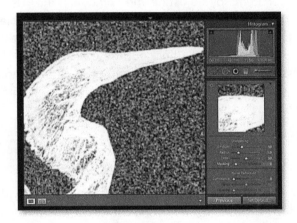

As you can see, the background and the bird both contain a lot of grain. Put another way, all of those locations undergo sharpening. Think about this image:

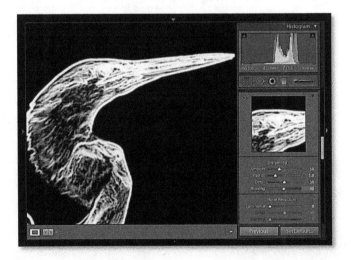

As I shifted to the right, the grain or dust in the sky disappeared, leaving just the bird visible. This essentially instructs Lightroom to only sharpen the bird and ignore the rest of the image. This is a fantastic method to enhance specific areas of a picture without altering the entire image.

Noise reduction and zoom

You can clearly see how Lightroom Classic's noise reduction settings operate when you view your image at a 1:1 zoom.

There are two methods for doing that: The Detail panel contains the first. A preview square with a 1:1 zoom is located at the top. Click the triangle on the right to reveal or conceal the preview square. Click and drag on the square to view a different area of the image.

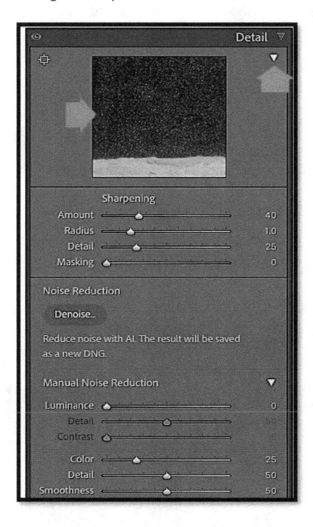

If the preview box is disabled and you aren't looking at the image at 100%, Lightroom Classic displays an exclamation point at the top of the Detail panel. To adjust Zoom to 1:1, click the symbol.

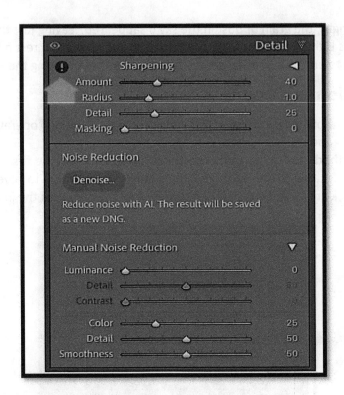

Manual Noise Reduction or Denoise?

Lightroom Classic included several sliders to reduce noise in your photos before the Denoise tool was introduced. Adobe has repositioned these next to Manual Noise Reduction at the bottom of the Detail panel.

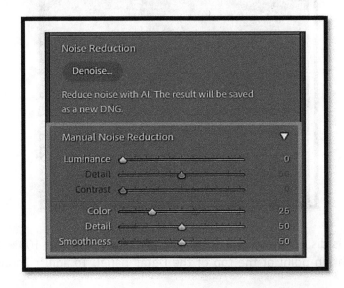

You must now choose between using the Manual Noise Reduction sliders or the new Denoise tool. Using the buttons by hand has the following benefits:

- All file kinds, including TIFF and JPEG, are compatible with them. Only raw files can be used with Denoise.
- They are faster. Depending on your computer's age and specifications, the Denoise tool may take 30 seconds to ten minutes or longer to operate.

When Luminance Noise Reduction is applied, the image becomes less detailed, which is the main issue with Manual Noise Reduction. Brightness noise cannot be eliminated without sacrificing sharpness. Luminance Noise Reduction is therefore by default set to 0. The fact that AI-based solutions like Denoise don't have this issue is another reason why they perform so effectively.

The advantage of employing Denoise is as follows:

- Without sacrificing any clarity, denoise performs a far better job of eliminating noise, including luminance noise.

Using Denoise has the following drawbacks:

- Depending on the specifications of your machine, the procedure takes longer (30 seconds to 10 minutes per photo). Because of this, using it to process more than a few photos in bulk is not feasible.
- Denoise requires additional storage space because it produces a new DNG file that can be up to four times larger than the original Raw file.
- Denoise can only be applied to images in the Raw and DNG formats. Although it isn't presently available, Adobe intends to expand the capabilities to JPEG and TIFF files.

I adore the Denoise tool despite its drawbacks. Here's an example to illustrate why. This is a picture I took at a concert at ISO 12,800.

The original image (on the left) and the updated image (on the right), created using the Denoise and Manual Noise Reduction options, are different. I simply showed you a little portion of the screen, so you can see the entire thing. The final result is excellent.

Therefore, I believe you should decide whether to utilize Denoise or Manual Noise Reduction for each shot separately due to the processing time. Use Denoise if you wish to maximize the quality of images that were captured at high ISOs and have visible noise. The wait was worthwhile, as you can see. In certain images, you should manually press the buttons.

How to Utilize Lightroom Classic's Manual Noise Reduction

To utilize the hand sliders, you must complete these procedures. Since each has its own sliders, we'll examine reducing brightness and color noise in Lightroom Classic one at a time.

Sliders for Luminance Noise Reduction

It's crucial to understand that before you use the Luminance tool, Luminance Noise Reduction will eliminate details from the image. You've probably noticed that JPEGs from smart phones taken in low light appear rather blurry. Brightness noise reduction operates in this manner. The brightness noise reduction parameter is by default set to zero to prevent this. Most of the time, it's best to leave it there. However, gradually increase the amount if you do use it. Start by adjusting the scale to 5 or 10 instead of 30 or 60. Some detail may be lost due to luminosity noise reduction. The Detail tool can be moved to restore it. To restore any lost contrast, slide the Contrast bar. An example window portion of a photograph with brightness noise at 1:1 zoom is displayed in the pictures below. The softness of the settings for Luminance 0 and Luminance 20 differs significantly.

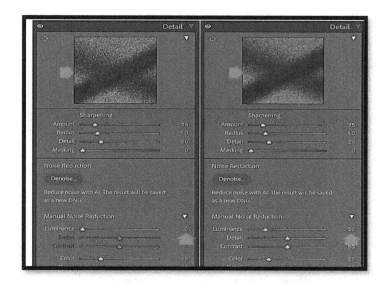

Sliders for Color Noise Reduction

Color noise is reduced with the Color slider. By gradually blurring the image, it accomplishes the same goal. The default value for the Color slider is 25. There may be color noise in this setting. Move the bar to the right until it disappears if it does. The Detail scale restores the detail that was lost in the process. It comes with a setting of 50. The Smoothness tool smoothes out any noise produced by the Color and Detail sliders. Since the effect is so slight, it takes a lot of movement to notice a change. The setting is 50 as before. Here's another illustration. When color noise reduction is adjusted to either 0 or 100, the same image is displayed.

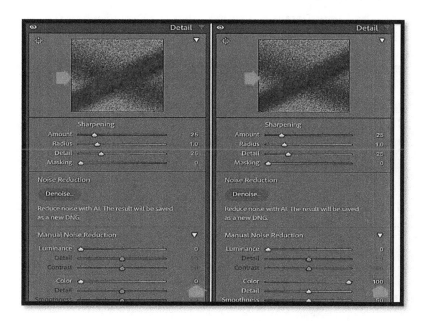

Finding the sweet spot where the bar is as far to the left as it can go while still eliminating all color noise is the goal when it comes to color noise reduction.

Dealing With Denoise

Before we go into the specifics of the Denoise tool, let me demonstrate how to utilize it. Keep in mind that it only functions with unprocessed Raw files (more on that below). PSD, TIFF, and JPEG files are not compatible with it.

- Click the Denoise button in the Detail panel to get started.

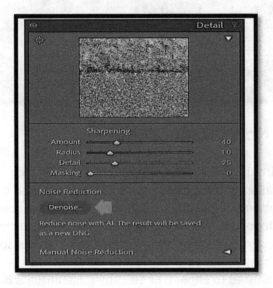

- The Denoise and Raw Details boxes are already checked when the Enhance Preview window opens.

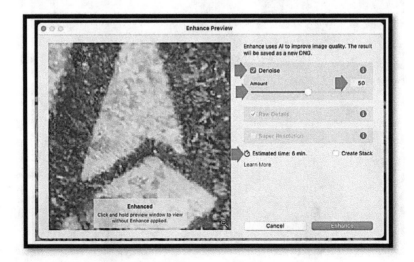

64

All you have to do is move the slider for amount. To add more Denoise, move the value to the right; to remove some, move it to the left. 50 is the typical setting. I think 50 is an excellent setting because it eliminates noise without making the image appear overly smooth. Lightroom makes an educated judgment as to how long handling the file will take. The size of your image, the age of your machine, and the speed of your graphics card all affect how long it takes. My iMac, which is six years old, gives me times of roughly six minutes. On a more recent machine, these times might not take long. On a slower computer, it may take much longer (see below for strategies to deal with this). You won't be able to experiment with different Amount values if your machine takes a long time to apply Denoise, as mine does. This is just one more compelling argument for leaving the setting at fifty.

- Click the Enhance button to get started. Lightroom appends Enhanced-NR.dng to the end of a new DNG file and employs both Denoise and Raw Details.

This image demonstrates Denoise's strength. On the left is a 100% enlarged image of a photo captured at ISO 12,800. The effect appears on the right when you use Denoise with the Amount set to 50.

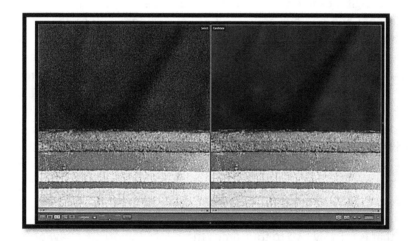

The details are still present, but the noise level has decreased. Lightroom employs the Raw Details tool in addition to Denoise, which is why there is even more detail visible. Compared to the "old" way of applying Luminance Noise Reduction in Lightroom, which softens the image and eliminates information, this is a huge improvement.

Everything you should know about Denoise

Even if you now understand the fundamentals, there are still a few things you should know about Denoise.

- Denoise is not required for every image. First, that might take too long. Secondly, it is not yet compatible with JPEG, TIFF, and PSD files. You can still use the previous Noise Reduction settings in those situations. They are now located at the bottom of the Detail panel and are referred to as Manual Noise Reduction.

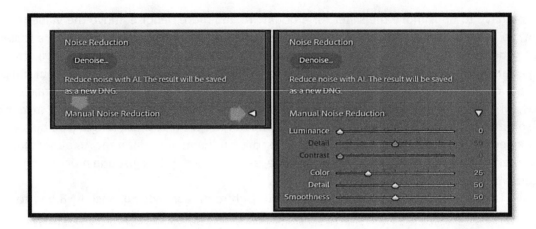

- As of this writing, Denoise is limited to Raw files from cameras having an X-Trans sensor (found in the majority of Fujifilm X series cameras) or a Bayer array (found in the majority of digital cameras). DNG files can also be created with the Adobe program or the Lightroom app on your phone. All of your camera's mosaiced data is preserved in these Raw files, which is necessary for Denoise to function.

- The smaller Raw files that certain cameras provide, such as Canon's sRaw, are incompatible with it. Additionally, it is incompatible with ProRaw iPhone files created by the iPhone Camera app. Because the camera processed some of the data and saved it in a manner that Denoise cannot read, it is unable to work with these Raw files.Additionally, the Lightroom app on your phone and uncompressed DNG files created by Adobe software are compatible with it. However, lossy DNG files, which have been de-sampled like the Raw files we previously discussed, do not work with it.

- Adobe has not yet stated when Denoise will be able to function with additional file types, such as JPEG, although they plan to do so shortly.

- When you use Denoise on a shot, Lightroom creates a new DNG file called Enhanced-NR.dng that is roughly two to four times the size of the original Raw or DNG file.

- You can apply the Denoise effect to multiple images in the Filmstrip at once if you select them and click the button. Please avoid selecting too many images at once, as this can prolong the process.

- Before using Healing or AI masking, it is advised that you utilize Denoise. AI-driven tools, such as Content-Aware Remove and AI masking, work best when they begin with a blank slate because noise can interfere with their functionality.

- Lightroom will update and modify any prior AI masks or Content-Aware Remove settings if you apply Denoise to an image that already has them. Additionally, it takes more time to verify the outcome to make sure everything is in order. Adobe advises you to run Denoise first because it creates more work for you.

- By adding Grain in the Effects tab, you can alter the outcome if you feel it is too smooth.

- You get the best of both worlds because the picture is simultaneously treated with both denoise and raw details. However, Super Resolution and Denoise cannot be applied to the same image.
- For optimal performance, Adobe recommends a GPU (Graphics Processing Unit) with at least 8GB of RAM and updated drivers.

Lens Corrections Panel Operation

Although the Lens Corrections box in Lightroom Classic appears to be simple, there is a lot going on behind the scenes. You don't have to give it much thought most of the time. Simply be sure you check the appropriate boxes before developing your images. However, it's not always the case that things go as planned. At that point, knowing more about it is beneficial.

What is the purpose of the Lens Corrections Panel?

Chromatic aberration, vignetting, and optical distortion caused by the camera lens are eliminated or reduced in Raw files using the Lens Corrections panel (although not in JPEGs, which may already have been rectified in the camera). The Profile and Manual tabs are located in the Lens Corrections panel. The Profile tab in Lightroom is where you can locate and utilize lens profiles.

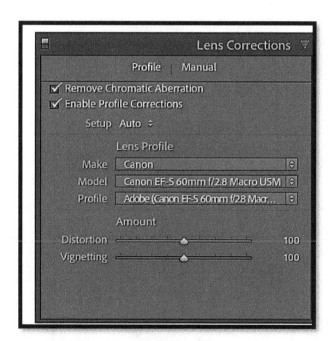

You can choose the amount of vignetting reduction, chromatic aberration reduction, or distortion correction you wish to perform yourself under the Manual tab.

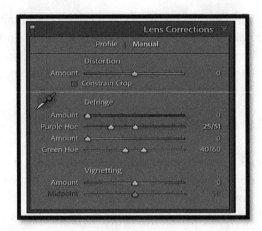

Eliminate Chromatic Aberrations on the Profile Tab

A color border that appears around the borders of an object in a photograph is known as chromatic aberration. When the subject is light from behind, older wide-angle or zoom lenses are likely to produce color swirls around the frame's edges. They could be blue/yellow, red/cyan, or purple/green. To see them, you usually have to zoom in 100%. The image below shows some color fringing around the borders of the tree stems at 100% zoom.

Go to Remove Chromatic Aberration and check the box to get rid of them.

Enable Profile Corrections using the Profile Tab

Vignetting, barrel distortion, and pincushion distortion are all fixed using profile corrections. Occasionally, the frame's sides are darker than its center. Vignetting is the term for this. Vignetting typically appears at a lens's widest aperture settings. It gradually disappears as you slow down. A 50mm f1.8 lens was used to take the image below. The unfixed version, complete with vignetting, is on the left. On the right is the fixed form without vignetting.

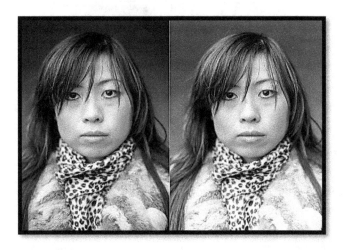

The one with the background looks better in this instance. You can alter how Lightroom Classic corrects vignetting if that suits you better. Straight lines are bent outward by the lens to resemble a barrel's sides. We refer to this as barrel distortion. You may purchase it with both fixed and zoomed wavy lenses. A low-quality lens is more likely to cause barrel distortion. This image was captured using a zoom lens that was 18–135 mm.

The difference between this form and the previous one is evident.

Pincushion distortion is the inward curvature of straight lines. Unlike barrel distortion, you usually won't notice it until you look for it, but it can occur with some zoom lenses. Since it's so uncommon, I don't have any cases to show you.

The Built-in profiles

The message "Built-in Lens Profile" may appear at the bottom of the Lens Corrections panel, depending on the camera and lens combination you have.

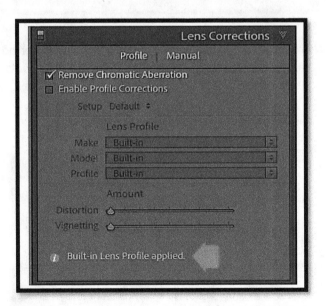

This indicates that a lens setting that your camera stored in the Raw file is being used by Lightroom. It frequently occurs with small cameras. That's fantastic if this describes you! The work was done for you by your camera. There is no use in searching for lens profile because it is not there in the Lens Corrections panel. If you haven't previously, tick the Enable Profile Corrections box. If Lightroom detects the correct lens profile in the image's EXIF data, it utilizes it right away. The lens type may not always be detectable by Lightroom. You can then manually select it from the available options. Because they are too old or haven't been profiled by Adobe, some lenses could not be in the database. In that scenario, a profile might already be applied to the Raw file, displaying the message "Built-in Lens Profile applied."

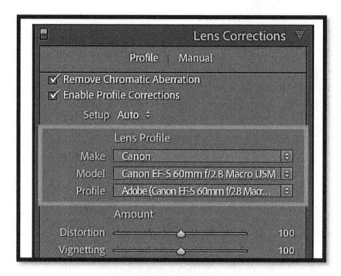

The sliders below allow you to adjust the amount of distortion or vignetting that is fixed. They're both already at 100. A slider can be moved to the left to make the adjustment weaker or to the right to make it stronger.

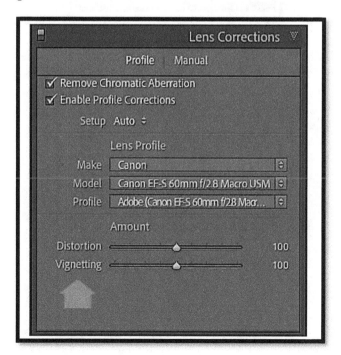

For photos like the one above, where the frame enhances the image, this works great.

How to Use the Lens Corrections Panel to Set a Default Lens Profile

Lightroom determines the type of lens used by analyzing the EXIF information in the image, but it only applies a profile if it is certain of the lens type. You can select a setting on your own (as long as it exists) if Lightroom doesn't apply one. You can set it as the default profile for that lens if you don't want to select it every time. You do it like this.

- Select the desired camera or lens profile in an image in the Develop module, then select the "Enable Profile Corrections" box. Make sure Lightroom doesn't automatically assign it a lens setting.

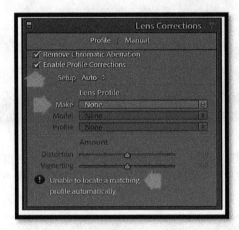

- Select the profile you wish to modify using the options after checking the box next to Allow Profile Corrections. If necessary, you can adjust the Vignetting and Distortion sliders.

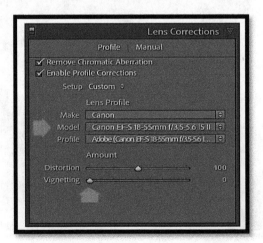

⁜ Next, under the Setup menu, choose Save New Lens Profile Defaults.

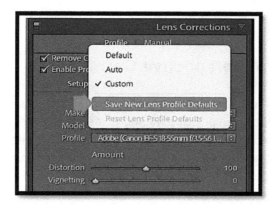

⁜ The next time you open a photo taken with the same camera and lens, Lightroom will utilize the profile you just specified as the preset if you set the Setup menu to preset. Also, if you altered the vignetting and distortion settings.

The Lens Corrections panel's Setup menu

There are three settings in the Setup menu.
   ⁜ **Default:** Allows you to alter the parameters for a particular lens.
   ⁜ **Auto:** Allows Lightroom to look for a profile that matches.
   ⁜ **Custom:** This indicates that a profile was chosen by hand or that a setting (such as the Vignetting slider) has been altered.

Manual Tab

Go to the Manual tab if your lens does not already have a profile or if you choose to modify or disregard the profile settings. This is typically the result of not fully eliminating all chromatic aberrations when the box next to Remove Chromatic Aberrations was checked.

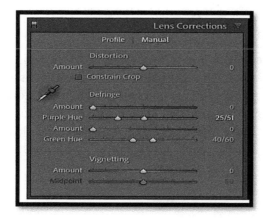

The Distortion and Vignetting sliders allow you to create your own distortion corrections or adjustments. To manually eliminate chromatic aberrations, select the eyedropper icon and then click on the remaining color bands in the image. You can also manually move the buttons if necessary.

Transform Panel for Perspective Corrections

When using a wide-angle lens to snap a photograph of a building, it is crucial to keep the camera straight. Even a slight tilt alters the perspective and is seen in the image. I can't keep the camera straight all the time; therefore I constantly have this problem. This image illustrates my point. I made it with a 17mm lens and an APS-C camera. I had to tilt the camera back slightly to get a better view of the residences. The houses are distorted as a result. To be clear, the green house on the right appears to be on the verge of collapsing.

In Lightroom Classic, you can correct the skew by navigating to the Transform panel. Naturally, you should make every effort to perform it flawlessly in front of the camera. Although the Transform panel is helpful, it reduces your image by half. It's a good idea to give extra space around the corners of the frame to accommodate this.

The panel for lens corrections

Prior to using Profile Corrections on your photo, navigate to the Lens Corrections panel. Proceed to the Transform panel after that. That's because barrel distortion is a common feature of wide-angle lenses. Barrell distortion is the appearance of straight lines stretching outward, such as the sides of a barrel. Sometimes the changes are so subtle that you have to perform a profile correction before you see them. The Profile tab has two boxes. It reads "Remove Chromatic Aberration," and it reads "Enable Profile Corrections." Check these boxes and select the lens setting if Lightroom doesn't locate it right away.

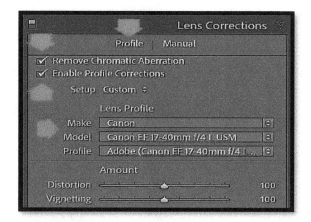

Lightroom Classic detects and fixes any chromatic flaws in your image, as well as applying the lens profile to eliminate any vignetting and distortion caused by the lens. If you're not satisfied with the results, you may use the Distortion and Vignetting sliders at the bottom to reverse Lightroom's alterations, or you can select the Manual tab for further options. If Lightroom Classic displays the phrase "Built-in Lens Profile applied," it means that your camera's software has applied a built-in profile. Since there isn't a profile for your lens in Lightroom's library, you don't need to click Enable Profile Corrections, despite this popup telling you to. Mobile cameras typically do this.

The Upright Tool and the Transform Panel

Next, navigate to the Transform panel and utilize the Upright tool (shown below).

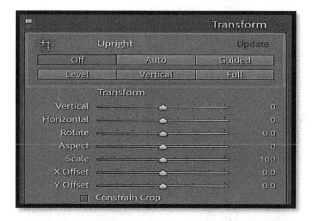

Off, Auto, Guided, Level, Vertical, and full are all buttons you can press. You may adjust the size, angle, vertical and horizontal location, and X and Y offsets using the seven parameters located beneath each button. These sliders can be used to adjust Lightroom's settings, or you can simply use them instead of the Upright tool. However, you won't need to touch them frequently. Note:

The sliders are arranged differently in Lightroom 6 and the Guided button is absent. Pressing the "Auto" button should be your initial action to test if it corrects the image." You won't need to press another button because the Auto button will perform admirably most of the time. When Auto was in use, the image above looked like this. To correct it, the image was cropped little, but now it looks much better.

If Auto doesn't function well enough or you're just curious, you can try the Level, Vertical, or Full buttons to see if these improve things.

- **Level:** Adjust any distortion from left to right, but not from top to bottom.
- **Vertical:** Corrects distortion from left to right as well as up and down. Compared to Auto, this button is probably going to produce better results for you.
- **Full:** Usually applies a severe crop, but applies the highest degree of distortion correction in all directions.

The buttons below can also be changed if necessary. I won't go into too much detail here because you won't need to touch these sliders very often and you can see what they do when you change them.

Guided Tool

Alternatively, you might utilize the Guided tool and complete it by hand. All you need to do is draw lines on the image to indicate the locations of the straight lines. As an example, let's examine the image below, where the straight lines are joining.

The screen illustrates how it operates. In the first, I sketched a line along a vertical line that was merging in the image. You can see exactly where you've set the line by using the loupe that Lightroom displays (if you don't see it, select the Show Loupe box in the Toolbar).

On a separate vertical line, I then drew a second line. Both lines are visible in the image below. You can draw lines left and right as well as up and down.

Lightroom will correct the image itself after you've drawn two or more lines. You can add more lines, if necessary, but this time the outcome was flawless. Additionally, you can alter the outcome by pressing the buttons at the bottom.

Hint: Check the Constrain Crop box to remove the white area surrounding the image.

Significant Modifications to the Transform Panel

Last but not least, this is an illustration of an extremely drastic Transform panel alteration. First, this is a photo I took with a wide-angle lens, intentionally turning the camera back to display the tall, vibrant buildings against the deep blue sky and create the illusion of lines overlapping.

This is what I get if I go to the Transform panel and click the Auto button. The dwellings were straight, yet that crop was large.

This could be useful if you want to experiment with similar-looking images.

CHAPTER SIX
EXTENSIVE EDITING METHODS

Graduated Filter

Lightroom has a versatile tool called the Graduated Filter that allows you to make minor adjustments to an image. With the help of this tool, you may progressively apply various effects to specific areas of an image. This filter is typically used to alter the sky's color or the edges' brightness or blackness in an image. In the following section, you will discover how to utilize Lightroom's graded filter. Additionally, there are some helpful hints to help you get the most of this tool. In Lightroom Classic, select the image you wish to enhance. To darken the sky in my countryside photo, I'll apply the Lightroom Graduated Filter.

- **Turn the Graduated Filter on:** Once the picture has been imported, select the Develop Menu. Click on the Graduated Filter icon beneath the Histogram. Upon pressing the button, a menu resembling the "Basic" panel will appear, featuring sliders to adjust exposure, color temperature, and other settings. When you move the mouse to the image, it changes to the "+" symbol.

Advice: Press the "M" key on your computer to access the Graduated Filter.

- **Set the Filter on a Picture:** Press and hold the left mouse button while moving the cursor over the image to apply the filter. The Graduated Filter transition will alter the distance between your initial click and the point at which you release the mouse, as well as the angle at which you move the mouse. Applying the gradient filter from top to bottom, left to right, or any other angle is possible with this tool. When you have finished creating the line for the effect, simply release the mouse button. Tip: To make drawing a straight line simpler, use the Graduated Filter and hold down "Shift" while moving the mouse. Depending on whether you're using the filter top to bottom or left to right, this will assist you in drawing a straight line at 0o or 90o.

- **Adjust for Position:** Even after you've finished drawing, Lightroom allows you to adjust the filter. You can drag a line to adjust its location. Additionally, you can tilt the filter by dragging the mouse pointer over the circle that appears inside the effect to reveal two arrows. Next, tilt the gradient by clicking and dragging the mouse. In Lightroom, the rotation handle will show up when you place the mouse pointer on the middle line of a graded filter, making it simple to spin the filter. Pressing it will allow you to adjust the effect as you see fit. To see the precise region where the effect will be applied, use the "O" key to make the covered area stand out in red. Press "Shift" and "O" to alter the mask's color if the image obscures the designated area.
- **Modify the Configuration:** After positioning the Graduated Filter as you like, return to the menu on the right and adjust the sliders to achieve the desired effect. The Basic panel's settings and this one are essentially identical. If you want to create a Graduated Filter Lightroom look with neutral sharpness, reduce the brightness. Conversely, you can blur out portions of the image using the sharpness setting. This step is necessary if you want a tilt-shift effect or a shallow depth-of-field appearance. A tip is to go to the

Adjustment menu, choose "Brush," and then choose "Erase" if you want to undo your adjustments.

- **Include Color Effects:** In Lightroom, you can also alter the filter's color. Select a color from the chart by pressing the color box located at the bottom of the filter panel. Move the mouse around until you discover a color that complements the shot. By shifting the scale beneath the color chart from left to right, you can adjust the color's brightness if you like the tone.
- **Completed**

Using a Radial Filter

The Radial Gradient tool in Adobe Lightroom Classic 2025 is essential for photographers who need to perform accurate localized adjustments. This application allows users to make targeted adjustments that highlight specific areas of an image by creating elliptical or circular masks.

The Radial Gradient Tool's Access

To begin utilizing the Radial Gradient tool in Lightroom Classic, navigate to the Develop module. Upon arrival, locate the Masking icon beneath the Histogram. A collection of masking tools is

displayed when you click this button. From this list, select the Radial Gradient option   . Shift + M can be used to fast open the tool if you prefer to utilize computer keys.

Establishing and Placing a Radial Gradient

With the Radial Gradient tool chosen, click and drag the area of the image you wish to modify to create the gradient. The gradient's center is set by the initial click point, and its size and form are altered as you go outward. By default, the gradient assumes the shape of an ellipse, but by holding down the Shift key while dragging, you can make it adhere to a perfect circle. You can adjust the gradient's size and direction by dragging the white handles around its edges once you've set it. This enables you to align the gradient exactly with the desired changing area.

Setting Up the Affected Area

Knowing which aspect of the image the change will impact is crucial. By default, all modifications only impact the region outside the gradient. To flip this selection and make sure that modifications only impact the region inside the gradient, just click the flip box in the Masking panel. Additionally, the Feather slider modifies the degree of softness of the shift between the modified and unmodified sections. While the lines between the colors stand out more when the feather value is lower, a greater feather value makes the mix smoother and more natural.

Making Adjustments

Once the Radial Gradient is properly positioned and set up, you can make several adjustments to the area you have selected. The sharpness, color, contrast, brightness, and other elements can all be altered. Raising the brightness inside the gradient, for instance, can highlight a topic, while lowering the saturation outside the gradient can lessen the saturation of the backdrop and increase the prominence of the primary figure.

Real-World Uses

There are numerous creative applications for the Radial Gradient tool because of its great versatility. It is frequently used by photographers to highlight items by highlighting specific areas, which directs the viewer's interest. It also works well for creating non-centered bespoke vignettes, which allows you to highlight non-center elements. The program gives users a lot of choices for enhancing photographs by enhancing the sky, adding warmth to certain areas, and even simulating lighting effects.

Extra Advice: Users who might not be able to see the gradient guidelines while using the tool can precisely place and alter them by using the H key to toggle their appearance. When you wish to adjust the gradient's position and effect, this option is helpful. By mastering the Radial Gradient tool in Adobe Lightroom Classic 2025, photographers may have greater control over their edits. This enables them to make minor yet discernible adjustments that raise the overall caliber of their images.

Tool for Spot Removal: Cloning and Healing

Dust spots that appear in images can be effectively removed with Lightroom's spot removal feature. But that's not all! You can get rid of plugs and plants in addition to humans. You'd be shocked at how much you could get rid of with Lightroom's spot removal tool. It combines the functions of a healing brush and a clone tool. This implies that you can repair, restore, or duplicate your images without bringing them inside Photoshop. Lightroom is where you can do it everything. In my opinion, anything that speeds up the editing process is beneficial. Although it's really simple to use, there are a few tips to make the most of it. Let's first examine how to remove simple spots using Adobe Lightroom Classic.

What is the purpose of the spot removal tool?

As the name suggests, to get rid of spots. It's not just about the skin. Another option is to eliminate:
- A bee buzzing through the picture while photobombing
- Wall markings in an image's background
- Spots, wounds, bruises, and patches of glossy skin
- Clothing stains from chocolate ice cream
- Background text and graffiti
- Reducing wrinkles
- Illuminating the shadows behind the eyes
- Clearing out trash of all sizes from fast food boxes to cigarette butts
- Streetlights, telephone cables, and poles
- Individuals can also be eliminated.

The list is endless. Because websites frequently position exit and no smoking signs in the wrong locations, making them seem terrible in the backdrop, I've used it a lot for wedding photos. Plugs and fire extinguishers function similarly. I've used digital tools to clean kids' noses, iron out fabric wrinkles, and remove loose threads from clothing (at 100% magnification that made my stomach heave a little). It's also a fast method for removing lens flare-induced sun blotches from photos.

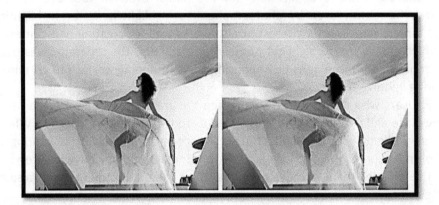

An instance of digital purification! Avoid folding and storing photographs that employ airy textiles. To prevent them from developing straight line creases between shoots, group them together instead.

Eliminating Sensor Dust Symptoms

Lightroom's spot removal tool is excellent for eliminating black smudges in photos that result from dust and debris on the camera. This is demonstrated by Lightroom's Visualize Spots function, which meticulously eliminates sensor dust spots.

Using the Spot Removal Tool for Cloning

Thus far, we have shown that the spot-removal tool may be used to clone portions of an image and add items. For instance:
- Thickening the foliage
- Making a thin hair patch thicker
- Fixing a patchy lawn
- Adding a button to an upholstered sofa that is missing

The tough aspect is that sometimes the best location edit to utilize to replicate anything is heal, not clone.

Where is Lightroom's spot removal function located?

A row of buttons appears near the top of the panel on the right, immediately below the histogram, when you launch Lightroom's Develop Module. The second button from the left is the spot removal tool.

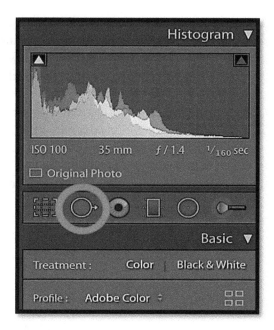

Click the icon to start the spot eradication process. You can open the spot tool and navigate to the Develop Module simultaneously if you hit Q on your PC while in any portion of Lightroom. The fact that shortcut keys speed up your job is their best feature! It's acceptable if you initially have trouble remembering them all. If you use Lightroom frequently and make an effort to use the shortcut keys frequently, you'll remember them better.

How Does the Spot Removal Tool in Lightroom Operate?

There are two methods to use the Lightroom spot removal tool:

1. Clone
2. Heal

I'll go over the differences between them and when to use each one because they are all helpful in different ways. But as I mentioned earlier, the heal feature is typically the best option. As we go over the features and demonstrate how to perform spot removal, we'll show you why.

Three sliders to adjust will appear when you choose the spot removal tool:

1. Size: Modify to encompass the desired repair area.
2. Feather: modify to soften the area's edges for a more seamless transition.
3. Opacity: not all substitutes must be completely opaque (more on this in a bit).

The image will become a white circle if you move your mouse pointer over it while the spot removal tool is selected. An inner circle might also be visible. As you adjust the feather setting, this will vary. There won't be an inner circle when the value is zero because there won't be any feathering.

To fix an area, click on it: An arrow pointing back to the location you selected will immediately appear elsewhere on the image, along with another circle of the same size and form. Lightroom will automatically select the area you wish to repair. I don't think it chooses the greatest position most of the time.

Choosing a different region

Simply click on it and drag it to a more convenient location. The arrow connecting the sample area and the region that requires fixing makes it simple to determine which is the sample area and which one requires copying. You can make as many changes as you like after you click on the area you wish to modify. Even the area's brightness, feather, and size can be altered.

Markings for hiding and revealing spot removal

A gray pin or a white circle will appear in the Develop module to indicate that spot removal has been applied to a specific area. Because these marks can interfere with your ability to change, it's useful to be able to conceal them. When you're ready, show them once more.

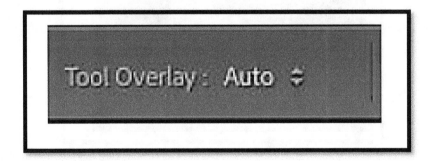

The menu, located in the lower left corner of the image, contains the Tool Overlay option. You can choose:

- Auto
- Always
- Selected

⚜ Never

The "H" key on your computer can also be used to reveal or conceal the marks.

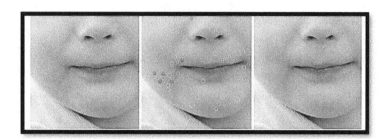

Wash your face digitally! Using the gray sticks, I "painted" a section by clicking and dragging them. I just selected an area by clicking on the white circles.

The spot removal tool's shape

If you click and drag the round spot removal tool over the area you want to correct, you may paint nearly any form you like.

What you must do is take out:
 ⚜ In the background are poles, telephone cables, and graffiti.
 ⚜ A hair that has fallen loosely across your subject's cheek or a wall crack.
 ⚜ A water puddle on the sidewalk.

A crucial piece of advice for repairing or cloning... Select an area on the same focus plane as the area you wish to correct for an invisible edit. If the area you select is less clear than the area you wish to correct, or vice versa, it will be more noticeable.

Examine specific areas of the image in the headline. Her hair, cosmetics in the corner of her eye (camera left), mascara under her eyelids (camera left), under-eye shadow on both eyes, and a few tiny places were all recreated by myself.

Four Situations in Which 100% Opacity Should Not Be Used

1. **Beneath Eye Shadow:** The spot removal tool is the fastest technique to lighten under eye shadow.
   - Make it roughly thirty percent opaque.
   - Click and drag over the area you wish to repair.
   - Click on the instantaneously created clone patch.
   - Position the patch immediately beneath your eye shadow on a smooth area of your face.
   - Click "Release" and adjust the thickness as necessary.
2. **Wrinkles becoming softer:** I find that the same technique smoothes out wrinkles particularly frown lines. Just make sure the region you take from is near and resembles the lines.

I cloned a tiny region on her brow to the left of the glossy place, followed by a smaller region to the right of the spot that went in the center of the shine. These were both set to 50%.

3. **Diminishing Shine The shine can also be diminished via spot treatment.** Faces are spherical, so if you take a sample of non-glossy skin to correct a shiny spot, it probably won't be exactly the same form. By adjusting the spot reduction opacity to less than 100% (often between 35 and 50%), you can conceal your alteration.

Since it was difficult to see, I adjusted the opacity of the spot removal tool to 87% in order to remove the white backdrop and the white flowers around her head. For the grass sections, it is 90% opaque.

4. **Make the grass or foliage thicker:** I prefer to reduce the opacity and allow some of the source images to shine through in order to give the background vegetation a more full appearance. In this manner, I avoid having uniform patches of foliage. There is no predetermined plan; you must experiment to see what suits you the best.

Why Heal Is Frequently Superior to Clone

The selected region is precisely duplicated when you perform the clone spot edit. Even if the edge is feathered, this may result in a hard edge that contrasts with the rest of the image. Because the heal spot edit uses the patterns and tones from the selected region rather than exactly replicating them, the cloned area frequently blends in better.

The contrast varies in three distinct ways depending on whether the Visualize Spots slider is in the middle, all the way to the left, or all the way to the right.

Visualize Spots: An Excellent Method for Eliminating Sensor Dust

I've already instructed you to remove the sensor dust-related black stains from your photos. The "Visualize Spots" box has been introduced by Lightroom to the Develop module's toolbar, which is located beneath your image. On your computer, you can choose it quickly by hitting the "A" key. (I've included a list of all the easy techniques to remove spots at the end.) Only when the spot removal tool is open can the Visualize Spots tool be seen. When you select Visualize Spots, a black-and-white border will appear around your image. You can adjust the scene's brightness or darkness using the slider in the menu, which is located next to the selection. Dust patches that you might normally overlook are easier to see when the background is clear, like a blue sky, and the contrast is high.

Two Unknown Spot Removal Techniques

- **View of the Spot Removal Before and After:** The spot removal tool panel's bottom left on/off switch makes it simple to monitor the progress of your job. I don't get why you would need to do this frequently since you can either remove (or duplicate) something or it's not there. But just in case, you now know. Consequently, viewing your edit is better than erasing the spot and then reversing the deletion.

+ **The Impact of Cropping on the Spot Removal Tool:** If you need to crop an image in Lightroom, start by using the spot removal tool. Using the spot-removal tool near the edge of a previously cropped image creates a smear. It does this by sampling nearby pixels that are not in the clipped region.

Shortcut for Spot Removal How to Boost Your Workflow

Too many pictures to process? Using Lightroom's keyboard shortcuts will speed up the process. They save a great deal of time because it is far faster to hit a key on the computer than to move the mouse to an icon, click on it, and then go back to the image.

- Q – Open the spot removal tool in the Develop module (even if you're in the Library module)
- H – Hide and unhide spot removal pins
- A – Visualize Spots
- Alt – Delete spot (hold down Alt, move cursor over the spot you want to delete, your cursor changes to scissors, click and the spot will be deleted)
- [– Increase size of spot
-] – Decrease size of spot
- Shift and [– Increase feather
- Shift and] – Decrease feather

Using the Range Mask

Adobe Lightroom Classic has many powerful capabilities designed to allow photographers total control over how their images are edited. Among these, the Range Mask function is very useful for making accurate local adjustments. Using the Range Mask, users can target particular regions according to brightness or color values. This makes it simpler to make little adjustments that can significantly improve a picture's visual appeal.

Comprehending the Range Mask Function

A more sophisticated tool in Lightroom Classic, the Range Mask enhances the appearance of selections made with the Radial Filter, Graduated Filter, or Adjustment Brush. Its primary function is to enable photographers to restrict adjustments to particular color or brightness ranges within an image. When working on complex situations, where standard masking techniques might not be precise enough to make minor adjustments, this capability is quite useful.

Turning on the Range Mask

To utilize the Range Mask feature, follow these steps:
- **Choose a Local Adjustment Tool:** To begin, choose the Adjustment Brush, Graduated Filter, or Radial Filter from the Develop module's menu.
- **Apply the First Adjustment:** Use the selected tool to paint or draw over the area of the image that needs to be altered. Make a small modification now to view the impacted region.
- **Turn on the Range Mask:** Locate the Range Mask option at the bottom of the adjustment window after making the initial adjustment. Click on the dropdown menu and select either Color or Luminance to make the change you wish to make.

The Luminance Range Mask in Use

The Luminance Range Mask allows you to alter an image according to its brightness levels. In settings with a lot of contrast, when you might only want to alter the highlights or shadows without altering the overall image, this is particularly useful.
- **Configuring the Luminance Range:** After selecting Luminance, adjust the range of light levels you wish to utilize using the Range sliders. For instance, to make adjustments to only the darker areas, use the sliders to concentrate on the lower end of the brightness scale.
- **Smoothing the Selection:** By adjusting the feathering between the modified and unaltered regions, the Smoothness slider creates a smooth, edge-free shift.

Using the Color Range Mask

You can alter and concentrate on specific colors in an image by using the Color Range Mask. Because of this, it's ideal for circumstances in which you wish to enhance or modify specific colors without compromising other aspects of the picture.
- **Choosing the Target Color:** To select the target color, select the color you wish to change in the image using the Eyedropper tool from the Color menu. Holding down the Shift key allows you to click on several different locations to see a wider view of many colors.
- **Changing the Amount Slider:** This slider allows you to fine-tune the range of colors that your modification will effect and regulates the color selection's limit.

Useful Range Mask Applications

Because of its versatility, the Range Mask tool can be applied to a variety of editing scenarios, including
- **Improving Skies:** In outdoor photographs, brilliant skies can be made darker and more detailed with the Luminance Range Mask without altering the background.
- **Selective Color Adjustments:** You can alter only specific skin tones or clothing colors in images with the Color Range Mask, leaving other aspects of the scene unaltered.

🔸 **Emphasizing Details:** For close-up shots, the Range Mask allows you to carefully manage specific color or brightness ranges, which can assist highlight minute details.

Advice for Efficient Use

🔸 **Visualizing the Mask Overlay:** Press the "O" key to turn the mask overlay on and off. The impacted red areas will be displayed. You can use this image to assess the accuracy of your selection and make any necessary adjustments.

🔸 **Combining Range Masks with Other Adjustments:** To make editing more challenging, you may combine the Range Mask with additional local adjustment tools. For instance, you may maintain the overall tone balance while enhancing contrast in specific areas.

🔸 **Practice and experimentation:** Until you become proficient with the Range Mask feature, you must practice using it. Experiment with various parameters and combinations to see how they impact your images and create an editing method that suits you.

By including the Range Mask in your Lightroom Classic toolkit, you may make precise adjustments to your images that will enhance their quality. You may now fine-tune your adjustments in a way that was before difficult with Lightroom thanks to this functionality. This increases your creative control and boosts the overall impact of your images.

CHAPTER SEVEN
ABOUT PORTRAIT EDITING AND RETOUCHING
Skin Retouching

We want the skin on our faces to appear smooth when we take a self-portrait in Lightroom. You should put a lot of effort into improving the appearance of your face in your photo. Don't worry, if you read this, I'll show you how to remove acne, dark spots, and greasy skin from your face. I will now discuss four methods for smoothing your skin in Adobe Lightroom Classic: Radial Adjustment Brush, Texture, Reverse Clarity, and Clarity.

Technique No. 1: (Use the Clarity option in Lightroom)

The clarity tool is probably the one that most people are familiar with because it has been around for a while. It functions by increasing the contrast in your image, primarily in the mid-tones. The black point decreases and the whites brighten as I adjust the clarity scale. It essentially extends the histogram, as you can see if you look at the one on the right. As our histogram returns to normal, I can see that more whites are growing brighter and the shadows are getting lighter. Because contrast alters saturation, increasing sharpness also alters the skin tones' saturation. This gives images a slightly rough, punchy appearance that makes them appear zombie-like!We're not aiming for attractive skin tones in this instance.

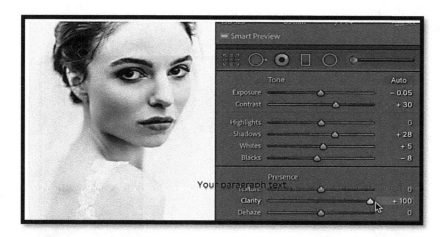

Technique No. 2: Soft Skin with Reverse Clarity

You can use the reverse clarity tool to easily edit your photos and get rid of those horrible pimples on your face, the darkness in your eyes and face, etc. Clarity used to be great because it raised contrast, but if we turn it around and lower contrast, it does the opposite. Despite this, it's still not ideal because it changes the color of the face by making the brightness higher.

Technique No. 3: Make use of the Texture Slider

(Step No. 1): This essentially replaces what I should do with Lightroom's clarity tool since Adobe recently added the texture scale. This is because the clarity tool only alters the mudstone texture's edge detail; if we zoom in a little more and experiment with his tool, I'll see if it allows us to either sharpen that, which looks very realistic, or remove it, which is best used for selective image editing.

(Step No. 2): Then, for our settings, the feature sets how soft the edges of your brush are, and I prefer to start with that at approximately 50. That gives us a beautiful soft edge without spilling. Let's reduce the roughness to 100% because I like it that way so you can see what you're doing.

(Step No. 3): Her skin isn't too awful, but as you can see, if we remove it and then add it back in, it merely gets softer. For an image like this, I would typically apply this step around step 30.

Technique No. 4: Color Adjustment Radial Brush

Radial Adjustment Brush: If you move the adjustment brush to the edge of our image, it will be applied to the entire image and the roughness will be reduced to -100. Next, we'll look at the mask option at the very bottom of the list and change this to a color. Next, we'll look at this small color picker, which allows you to select the various colors that are in that tone by holding down shift and moving your mouse over the various highlights, shadows, and mids of the face.

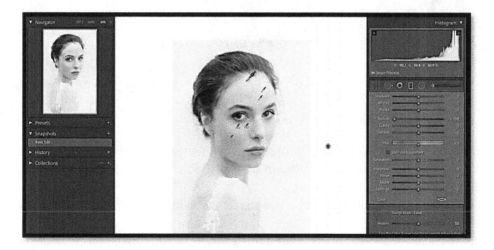

Using the Healing Brush

You should have tried to hide skin imperfections or get rid of dust or dirt from a photo, but if you haven't used Lightroom Classic's Healing Brush, this photo-fixing guide is a great place to start. The Healing Brush in Lightroom will save you a ton of time when you need to fix up photos, and the effects will do the talking.

The Healing Brush: What is it?

If you want to learn how to fix up photos, you'll need to know how to use Lightroom Classic's Healing Brush, which is a very helpful tool that can add and remove information from a specific area without any noticeable changes. In short, it has a powerful built-in algorithm that can remove unwanted details from your picture in a seamless manner.

How to Utilize Lightroom's Healing Brush

First, locate the Healing Brush tool. Lightroom makes this simple: locate the Healing Brush tool in the Develop module, directly beneath the Histogram. The shortcut appears as a band-aid; click on the bandage and select "Heal" from the Brush menu before you begin repairing photos.

Size, Feather, and Opacity are the three tools you can use with the Healing Brush; the settings you select for these will vary depending on how you edit images in Lightroom, but here's a broad idea:

- **Size:** When editing photos, pick a size that is just a bit larger than the detail you wish to eliminate.
- **Feather:** Select a lower number for a more accurate edit or a larger number for a softer edit.
- **Opacity:** Usually set at 100, this can be decreased if you wish to preserve a certain percentage of the information.

To eliminate a detail, select the Healing Brush and then enlarge it. In my example, I want to eliminate some crumbs from the lower left section of this image.

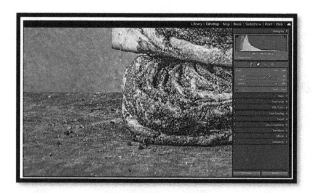

For this picture fix, click on the area you want to heal, and a second circle will appear; this is the Source Selection. As you adjust your healing brush, cut out a shape that shows what you want the Lightroom Healing Brush to use as the new pick that will replace the old one. I used a Brush Size of 78 to hide this small group of crumbs while I was fixing up the picture. The opacity stays at 100 because I want the crumbs to be gone forever, and the Feather is now 34.

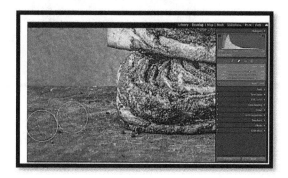

Now that Lightroom has employed the Healing Brush, it will seamlessly integrate the specifics of the source selection into our original selection. Let's examine how this photo correction technique actually operates.

You don't know. That's why the Lightroom Healing Brush is so effective at repairing images. After we made changes to our image in Lightroom, those parts vanished, leaving no trace of our work. That's how strong and user-friendly the Lightroom Healing Brush is.

Using the Healing Brush on a Portrait: A Guide

The Healing Brush in Lightroom is the ideal tool for this task, and the individual in the photo requested that we remove the tiny imperfection on their top lip after the photo shoot because they don't like it.

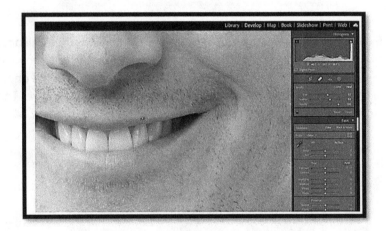

Since the teeth aren't in the picture we're correcting, I was cautious not to pick them. I set the Brush Size to 61 so that it only fits the lip and the freckle. To create a subtle falloff, I set the Opacity to 100 and the Feather to 69.

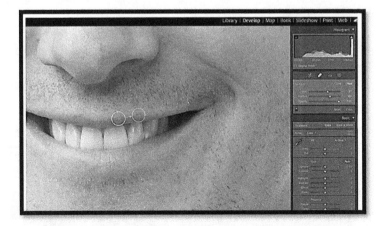

In the image you wish to correct, identify the source of the selection. I chose the area of the lip without any spots as my source.

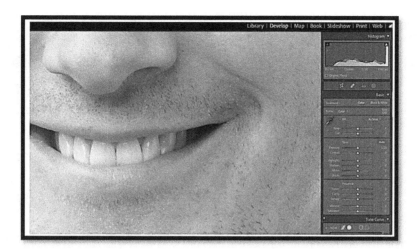

You now know how to utilize Lightroom's Healing Brush tool, which instantly removed the freckle and smoothed out our edit so that it appears as if the pimple never existed in the first place once the picture was corrected.

Whitening of teeth

Stage 1: Choose the Adjustment Brush

First, open the image you need to modify in the Develop module, then click the Adjustment Brush tool in the right panel or hit the "K" key on your keyboard to edit just specific areas of the image.

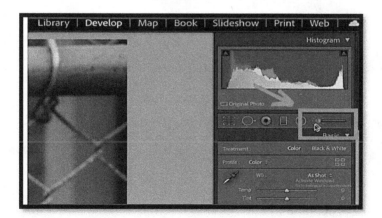

Stage 2: Select the Whitening Preset

In the Brush Adjustment panel, select the "Effect" panel and click the "Teeth Whitening" preset, which begins with the Saturation set lower and the Exposure set higher.

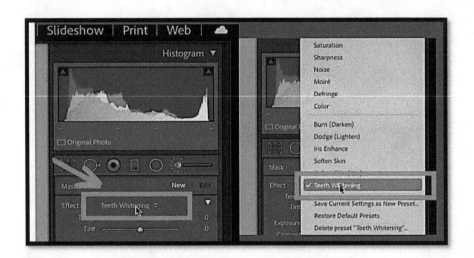

Stage 3: Adjust the Configuration as Necessary

If the setting is insufficient to eliminate significant color discrepancies, you can adjust the settings further:

Exposure: Increase up to +0.75 to brighten teeth.

Temperature: Decrease it to -20 to reduce yellow tones.

Saturation: Decrease -40 to -100 to remove color cast.

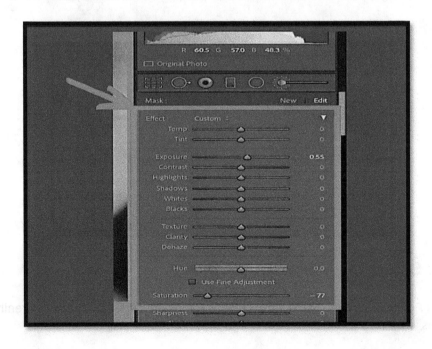

Stage 4: Configure the Brush

If you want to avoid going over the edges of your teeth, select "Auto Mask." For each tooth, adjust the brush size from 10px to 30px. Use 0–25 Feather for a crisp edge.

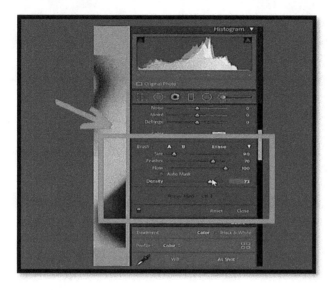

Stage 5: Cover the teeth with paint

To obtain a decent view, zoom in close on the teeth, use the brush to paint over each tooth, switch the mask layer so you don't go outside the lines, and use Erase if necessary.

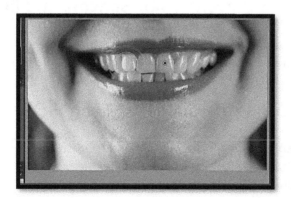

Stage 6: Examine and Adjust

Zoom out to see the full image, adjust the brightness as needed, take breaks to relax, and adjust the settings a bit till the brightness seems natural.

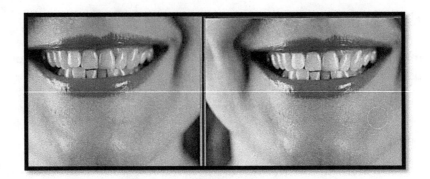

Stage 7: Save the Custom Preset

Click the Effect drop-down menu and select "Save current settings as new preset" to reuse the same settings repeatedly.

Seven Techniques to Whiten Your Teeth with Realistic Results

#1 Make Minor Modifications for a Natural Appearance

It's easy to go overboard and whiten your teeth too much, which will make them look very false and unnatural. To whiten your teeth softly, change the slider a little bit at a time, gradually increase the effect, and resist the urge to do too much. It takes time to achieve a natural look that is also enhanced.

#2 Complement the Current Color Scheme and Lighting

In order to fit the mood of the picture, the teeth's brightness and color cast should be realistic; for example, if the picture has melancholy, dark lighting and subtle tones, don't make the teeth extremely white and dazzling.

#3 Adjust the Brush Preferences for Each Picture

To get the greatest results, take the time to alter the brush settings, such as Exposure and Saturation, for each picture. The lighting, skin tones, degree of staining, and desired look will all vary, so don't use the same teeth-whitening brush setting on all of your photos.

#4 Start by isolating teeth whitening

Try bleaching the teeth first to avoid accidentally altering the skin tone or color and mood of the picture, then separate the modifications to the teeth and make additional edits before making any other global adjustments, including camera profiles, tone curves, or color grading.

#5: Cautiously Whiten Your Eyes

Lowering the Saturation and Temperature will naturally make your eyes appear whiter. Use the same Adjustment Brush tools to make your eyes whiter, but be careful not to add too much exposure, as this can create an artificial bright spot instead of reducing color.

#6 Examine Several Screens

Despite working up close, make sure you check the final image in full size on several screens because brightness and color might vary from device to device. Check the brightness on your laptop and mobile device to ensure it appears the same on both.

#7 Take pauses to get new insight

Spend some time focusing on specifics, but take frequent breaks to view the overall picture from a different perspective. Take a step back and make sure you haven't whitened too much because you could wind up changing too much if you get too wrapped up in the details.

Improving the Eyes

In headshot photography, enhancing the eyes can significantly improve the overall image. Adobe Lightroom Classic offers a collection of tools that photographers can use to enhance and brighten eyes while maintaining their natural appearance. This guide provides a comprehensive approach to eye brightening in Lightroom Classic to make sure your subjects' eyes catch the viewer's attention with clarity and brightness.

Preliminary Preparations

Prior to making eye-specific adjustments, you should do basic global alterations to your image to ensure that the overall exposure, contrast, and color balance are optimal, which will provide you with a solid foundation for improving individual areas.

Zooming in for accuracy

Zoom in on the subject's eyes for fine-tuning modifications; this close-up view allows for exact adjustments and ensures that the changes blend in with the rest of the image.

Making Use of the Adjustment Brush

The Adjustment Brush in Lightroom Classic is a versatile tool that allows you to alter particular areas of an image.
- **Adjustment Brush Activation:** Click the Adjustment Brush tool in the Develop module to begin using the Adjustment Brush.

- **Resetting Previous Settings:** To ensure that no inadvertent changes are made, double-click the "Effect" title to restore all sliders to their initial configurations.
- **Customizing Brush Settings:** Adjust the brush's size, feathering, and flow to suit the surface you're painting. A brush with mild flow and soft edges is typically ideal for eye enhancements.

Using Brightening Modifications

Once the Adjustment Brush is configured, proceed to lighten the eyes:
- **Improving Exposure:** To add light to the eyes, move the Exposure slider up a little. Be careful not to go overboard, since this might give the eyes an artificial appearance.
- **Boosting Highlights and Whites:** To bring out the eyes' inherent brilliance, gradually move the Highlights and Whites sliders.
- **Modifying Shadows:** To uncover hidden nuances, gradually raise the Shadows slider if the eyes seem shaded.
- **Refining Saturation:** Use the Saturation slider to slightly raise the iris color while keeping realistic tones in mind.

Improving Iris Specifics

To further highlight the pupils and draw attention to the eyes:
- **Improving Clarity:** Apply a tiny push to the Clarity tool to enhance the iris's texture and characteristics.
- **Sharpening:** To make the eyes appear clear and sharp, move the Sharpness tool to increase focus.

Taking Care of the Eye Whites

You can appear younger by brightening the sclera, or the whites of your eyes:
- **Lowering Saturation:** To minimize heat or color shifts, use the Saturation tool.
- **Temperature Adjustment:** To remove the yellow sclera, drag the temperature tool slightly closer to the blue end.
- **Lighting:** Increase the exposure gradually to brighten the whites, but take care not to increase it too much since this can make the sclera appear artificial.

Making Use of Presets to Increase Productivity

Lightroom comes with presets like "Iris Enhance" that you can use as a reference before you start working on your eyes.

To utilize these:
- **Choosing the Preset:** While the Adjustment Brush is still in use, you can choose the "Iris Enhance" setting from the Effect dropdown menu.
- **Applying and Modifying:** Use the eye settings and make any necessary adjustments to the sliders to achieve the desired look.

Final Evaluation and Modifications

Following the modifications:

- **Toggle the Adjustment:** Make sure the changes are limited to the designated regions by using the "O" key to toggle the mask overlay.
- **Compare Before and After:** You can evaluate the effect of your improvements by viewing the image before and after the adjustments by pressing the backslash key ("").
- **Adjust as Needed:** Make extra adjustments to guarantee that the eyes seem naturally brightened and harmoniously incorporated into the overall composition.

How to Avoid Burning and Dodging Black and White Images

In the studio, you had to place something between the projected negative and the paper (usually a piece of card on a stiff wire) to make some parts of the picture lighter, and you use a large piece of card with a hole cut in it to let more light hit part of the paper, which is where the term "burning in" originates. Yes, it all looks very outdated compared to Lightroom Classic, but the concepts are the same, even though the tools and means have changed. The first image we'll be working with today is this one, which I have already converted to black and white by setting the treatment to B&W, adjusting the tones in the B&W panel, and adding Clarity to bring out the texture.

Prior to Dodging and Burning

Now that we know what we want to do, we just need to figure out how to get it done. In this case, I started by making the watermelons on the outside darker. Before you start dodge and burn, you need to know what you want to do. I decided to make the watermelon in the middle a larger focus point when I took this picture.

Step 1: Burn in the edges with a radial filter

The watermelons are round, so it makes sense to use the Radial filter to make the outer ones darker, or "burn them in" in darkroom terminology. This is what happened when I placed a Radial Filter over the center of the watermelon and moved the Exposure scale to the left.

Some considerations about the Radial Filter are as follows:
- You can use the keyboard shortcut to view the mask that the Radial filter or any of the other local adjustment tools (Adjustment Brush, Graduated filters, etc.) creates; in Lightroom Classic, the mask appears as a red shape, and by adjusting the adjustment, the area that the mask covers changes, so it's not really a mask.

You can alter the mask's color by pressing Shift + O on your PC.
- You can adjust the feather tool's edge smoothness between the mask-affected area and the remainder of the image; the 50 setting appears to be a good fit; the shift becomes easier as the number increases and sharper as it decreases.
- By default, the mask is used outside the Radial Filter; to use it inside the circle, tick the "Invert" box.
- Holding down the Shift key while applying the Radial Filter to a picture causes it to change from a rectangle to a circle; when adjusting the filter's size, hold down the Shift key to maintain the height-to-width relationship.

Step 2: Burn the watermelon's center with a second radial filter

When I was making something, this shows you how to change your mind. You should have a plan, but you should also be open to other options as you work. I initially considered making the middle watermelon lighter, but I decided that it would look more interesting if I made it darker. I used an Invert Mask box to make the adjustment happen inside the filter rather than outside of it, and then I placed another Radial Filter on top of the fruit.

I shifted the Exposure tool to the left to make it darker, increased the Texture and Clarity levels to highlight the surface characteristics, and turned up the Highlights to make the image pop out a little.

This is how it ended up.

Use the Adjustment Brush or Graduated Filter to Dodge or Burn

Using the same principles, you may make minor adjustments using the Graduated Filter or Adjustment Brush, which is frequently used to alter the sky's brightness or darkness. Make sure the tool fits the form of the area you need to lighten or darken.

Use the Adjustment Brush tool when working with non-straight shapes, such as the man's hair and beard in this image.

Additional Examples of Dodging and Burning

Finally, we'll look at another example of dodging and burning, which is designed to give you an idea of how they thought about it. The how always follows the why, and you need to learn how to use dodge and burn to improve your shots before you decide which techniques to use.

Old car, Humahuaca, Argentina

This image of an ancient automobile in black and white has many beautiful textures.

When I used dodging to lighten the car's body, the background remained the same, and I simultaneously increased Texture and Clarity to highlight the best aspects of the faded picture.

I used the Adjustment Brush to create the mask.

Eliminating Flaws and Defects

I wanted to start a fresh article about using Lightroom to edit portraits because of its improved "healing brush" and new masking capabilities. Most individuals, in my opinion, are unaware of how much retouching they are capable of. I want to utilize this art to demonstrate that there is more that can be done now than ever before. **Let's start by discussing one of the most popular photo editing tasks: removing imperfections and reducing the size of objects like hot spots or scars.**

Step 1: This is our initial image. The new Content-Aware Remove brush will be used to eliminate imperfections. To access it, click the bandage-like icon in the toolbar near the top of the right-side panels. In the most recent version of Lightroom, this bandage is now known as the Healing tool instead of the Spot Removal tool. Press the first button when the "Mode" panel appears. We will only utilize the Content-Aware Remove brush going forward. Well, I don't like to say it, but the Heal brush is garbage.

Step 2: To get a close-up view of your subject's face, press Command-+ (or Ctrl-+ on a PC) a few times. Click and drag while holding down the Spacebar to move around the image. Remember, up here we can fix a few minor imperfections.

Step 3: Make your brush slightly larger than it is to get rid of a spot. The brush is made larger by the Right Bracket (]) and smaller by the Left Bracket ([). This can be done in the right-side panels of the Healing tool's settings panel, but using the Left and Right Bracket keys on your computer is more convenient. Use your mouse to highlight the area you wish to delete.

Step 4: Simply click again. That's all. As you can see, you don't need to "paint" with it; a single click should remove the place.

Step 5: Click once to eliminate the remaining defects in this section after completing the first four stages. Little dots that indicate where you used the brush have replaced your defects, so you can see that anything is wrong.

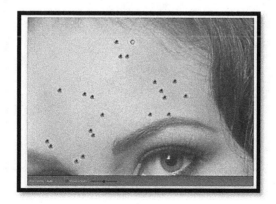

Step 6: Move your mouse outside the photo area and onto the panels on the right, as I did here, to check how your retouch appears. The icons will vanish for a brief period of time. I'm depressed about this. For this reason, I have to continuously move my mouse to the appropriate panels to see if the correction I made to the previous issue seems satisfactory. But we can solve that.

Step 7: Examine your image's gray Toolbar at the bottom. In the far left corner, you will notice the words "Tool Overlay." Press the letter T on your computer if you are unable to see the Toolbar. After that, click and hold to select "Never," as indicated below. You will now see the repair rather than the symbol when you move your cursor over a fault. This is how Photoshop's Healing Brush functions. Only when I'm using this brush does this setting change to Never. Upon finishing, I put it back to its default Auto show/hide configuration.

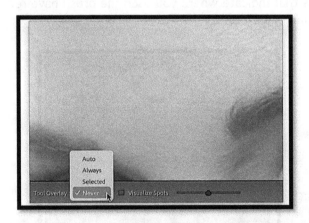

Step 8: To further scroll down, click and drag inside your image while holding down the Spacebar. Look for a few moles under her armpits on the right side of her neck. I usually don't remove moles because they are a part of the subject's personality. However, most retouchers reduce their prominence instead, as they are far more noticeable in photographs than in real life.

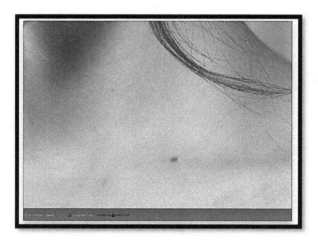

Step 9: To remove the spots, we'll employ the identical instrument and a comparable technique. Even though I stated that we wouldn't remove it, we are; we just need to go one more step. To completely eliminate the mole, move your mouse over it, resize the brush to be just a little bit bigger than it is, and then click once. Did you also note that there is no longer the obnoxious icon? The region that was repaired is visible inside the brush cursor. That's because I still have my Tool Overlay set to Never.

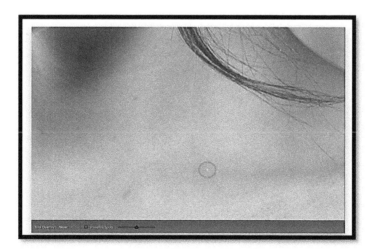

Step 10: Next, we'll adjust the Opacity's strength in the Healing tool's panel. This technique might be thought of as "Undo on a Brush." With it, we'll be able to "undo" part of the cleaning

that was done all around. The mole will return if you drag the Opacity to 0%, indicating that we did not remove it completely. If you leave it at 100% Opacity, it's gone. The mole begins to reappear as you adjust the tool to reduce the Opacity. Lowering it will keep it present but make it less noticeable and powerful. Here, I dropped Opacity by 36%, which restored most of it but not all of it. The mole has shrunk, but it is still there.

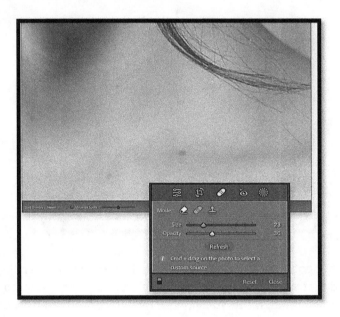

CHAPTER EIGHT

INTEGRATING LIGHTROOM CLASSIC WITH PHOTOSHOP

Configuring the Integration of Lightroom Classic and Photoshop

You get the best of both worlds when you combine Adobe Lightroom Classic's organizing features with Photoshop's robust editing capabilities. **Here's how to use and configure this integration correctly:**

- **Verify that both apps are installed:** First, confirm that your computer has both Lightroom Classic and Photoshop installed. If you need to install the apps on a different device, log into your Adobe account at adobe.com and download them.
- **Set up Lightroom Classic's External Editing Preferences:** To ensure seamless editing in both Lightroom Classic and Photoshop, set Photoshop as your preferred external editor.
  - ➢ Lightroom Classic should open.
  - ➢ Go to Lightroom Classic > Preferences (macOS) or Edit > Preferences (Windows).
  - ➢ Choose the tab for External Editing.
  - ➢ Click Choose under Additional External Editor, then find the Photoshop program on your PC.
  - ➢ For files edited in Photoshop, select your desired file format, color space, bit depth, and resolution. This setting ensures that a picture will open in Photoshop with the specified parameters when you open it in Lightroom Classic.
- **Use Photoshop to edit images from Lightroom Classic:** In PhotoShop, you can modify a photo shot with Lightroom Classic.
  - ➢ Choose the image you want to modify in the Develop or Library modules of Lightroom Classic.
  - ➢ Select Edit In > Edit in Adobe Photoshop [version number] by right-clicking the image.
  - ➢ Another option is to select Photo > Edit In > Edit in Adobe Photoshop [version number] from the menu. Once the image opens in Photoshop, you can use more simple editing tools.
- **Utilizing Lightroom Classic to store and modify edits:** After completing your Photoshop editing:
  - ➢ To save your work in Photoshop, select File > Save.
  - ➢ In Photoshop, you should close the file. To help you stay organized, the altered image will appear next to the original in Lightroom Classic right away.
- **Make Use of Complex Editing Processes:** Combining the two applications enables you to write using more sophisticated techniques:

- ➤ **Smart Objects:** To maintain editability and apply non-destructive filters, open photos as Smart Objects.
- ➤ **Panoramas and HDR:** Open a collection of images in Photoshop as layers to create panoramas or combine several exposures.
- ➤ **Compositing:** Make use of Photoshop's layering features to combine components from various photographs to produce composites. These sophisticated procedures provide you more creative options by combining the administration capabilities of Lightroom with the editing capabilities of Photoshop.

Using Photoshop and Lightroom Together for More Complex Editing

- ✦ **Lightroom's initial adjustments:** First, bring your RAW files into Lightroom. You may effectively arrange your photos with its robust tagging system. It is necessary to make simple adjustments like cropping, altering the brightness, and balancing the colors. Lightroom's non-destructive editing feature allows you to make improvements to your photographs while maintaining the integrity of your original files.
- ✦ **Moving Pictures to Photoshop for More Complex Editing:** You may easily transfer an image from Lightroom to Photoshop when it requires more intricate adjustments, including compositing, retouching, or the application of intricate effects:
  - ➤ To edit a picture in Lightroom, right-click on it and select Edit In > Edit in Adobe Photoshop. After opening in Photoshop, the image will be prepared for further processing. This connection enables you to leverage Photoshop's extensive toolkit for tasks that Lightroom is unable to perform.
- ✦ **Photoshop Advanced Editing:** Utilize Photoshop techniques such as these:
  - ➤ **Layering and Masking:** Combine many photos or portions, then use masks to determine which are visible.
  - ➤ **Retouching:** Use tools like the Healing Brush and the Clone Stamp to eliminate imperfections or unnecessary elements.
  - ➤ **Compositing:** Combine multiple images to create a scene that appears authentic. You may enhance the visual worth of your images by editing them with the aid of these capabilities.
- ✦ **Conserving and Getting Back into Lightroom:** After you've finished making modifications in Photoshop:
  - ➤ Choose File > Save to save the file.
  - ➤ In Photoshop, close the picture. To keep your work organized, the modified image will appear instantly next to the original in your Lightroom catalog.
- ✦ **Complete Modifications and Lightroom Export:** You can make any final adjustments to the altered image, such as lowering noise or brightening it, when you return to Lightroom. Once you're satisfied with the image, download it in the desired size and format. You can now print it out or share it. You may create a well-organized, potent procedure that increases your productivity and creativity by combining Lightroom's excellent organization with Photoshop's robust editing features.

CHAPTER NINE

LIGHTROOM CLASSIC FOR THE WEB AND PRINT

Getting Pictures Ready for Print: DPI and Color Spaces

To get the greatest results when preparing your photographs for printing in Adobe Lightroom Classic, you must closely monitor the color spaces and size settings. If you take proper care of these things, the duplicated images will have fine details and realistic colors, just like the ones you see on your computer.

Comprehending Lightroom Classic's Color Spaces

A picture's color space is the collection of colors it can display. Selecting the appropriate color space is crucial to ensuring that the colors seem consistent from screen to print. **In Lightroom Classic, the primary color spaces to consider are**

- **Adobe RGB (1998):** This color space can be utilized for professional printing where color accuracy and brightness are crucial because it offers a wider color gamut than sRGB. It is easier to create colors with more subdued tones since it covers a wider spectrum of colors, particularly in the cyan-green range.
- **sRGB:** Although it allows you to see fewer colors, this color space is frequently used for the web and general displays. Although some print providers will accept sRGB files, adopting this color space may result in less vibrant copies because it only supports a limited spectrum of hues.

When you export, Lightroom Classic will know what color space to utilize thanks to the following steps:

- Choose the image or images that you want to print.
- To enter the Export dialog box, select File > Export.
- Select JPEG or TIFF as the Image Format in the File Settings section.
- To print professionally, choose Adobe RGB (1998) from the Color Space dropdown menu.

You should inquire about the color space used by the print service you have selected. While some services can handle Adobe RGB, some may need sRGB files for better color rendering (1998).

Resolution Management: DPI and PPI

One of the most significant factors influencing the clarity and quality of your printed images is resolution. Digital image sharpness is commonly measured in pixels per inch (PPI). They display the number of pixels in an image per inch. A higher PPI typically results in a better image when printing. A printer uses that many ink dots per inch. We refer to this figure as dots per inch (DPI). PPI denotes the digital sharpness of the image, whereas DPI denotes the printer's output capabilities. Nonetheless, these terms are frequently used to describe the same phenomenon in

117

several contexts. Pictures with a sharpness of 300 PPI are typical. With this level, the image will have sufficient detail to print crisply and clearly.

To adjust the size while exporting in Lightroom Classic, follow these steps:
- Find the Image Sizing area in the Export dialog box.
- If you need to change the image's proportions, use the Resize to Fit option.
- Set the Resolution field to 300 pixels per inch and enter the desired measurements (such as width and height).

Making sure the resolution is correct is even more crucial when printing larger images because insufficient PPI might result in pixels and a loss of quality.

Extra Things to Think About When Printing

- **File Format:** TIFF files are frequently the best option for printing since they retain all of the image data without any compression issues and don't lose quality. However, high-quality JPEGs (with quality levels ranging from 77 to 85) are also frequently employed and can yield excellent results while maintaining manageable file sizes.
- **Output Sharpening:** You can improve the clarity of your prints by sending them with the proper sharpness settings. Choose "Sharpen For: Print." Next, select the paper type (Glossy or Matte) and desired sharpness level (Low, Standard, or High) under "Output Sharpening" in the Export box. The printing process sometimes makes things a bit too soft, but this step compensates for that.
- **Soft Proofing:** Lightroom's Soft Proofing tool allows you to preview how your images will appear on paper. Based on certain printer and paper profiles, this tool simulates the output. This enables you to tweak as needed to achieve the best print. To access Soft Proofing, navigate to the Develop module and choose the "Soft Proofing" box next to the image.
- **Monitor Calibration:** Regular monitor calibration ensures that the colors seen on your screen accurately reflect the image data. If you want the colors in your written findings and digital files to look the same, you must do this.

Print Module: Producing Eye-Catching Picture Books

- **Arrange Your Pictures**
  - To begin, select the images you like to utilize and arrange them as follows:
  - Create a Collection: In the Library module, select the images you wish to use and add them to a new collection. This makes it easier for you to manage and arrange your photos.
- **Go to the Book Module**
  - When your collection is prepared:
  - To access the Book module, click on it at the top of Lightroom Classic. The images you selected will appear at the bottom of the filmstrip.

Set Up the Book Settings
- ➢ First, arrange the fundamental elements of your book:
- ➢ **Book Settings Panel:** For instance, you can select a JPEG, PDF, or Blurb Photo Book as your book type. Additionally, you can select the paper grade, cover type, and size. You have a number of options with Blurb, including lay-flat and standard paper.

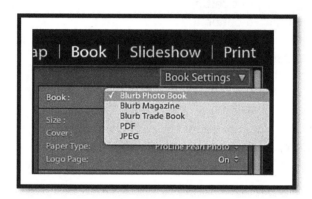

- **Create Your Layout:** Modify the appearance of your book:
  - ➢ **Auto Layout:** Using pre-configured models, this function enables you to quickly fill in your book.
  - ➢ **Manual Layout:** For a more customized look, use the Manual Layout option to select from a variety of page layouts and drag and drop images onto particular pages.
  - ➢ **Page Panel:** To prevent layouts from repeating, select whether and where to put page numbers and construct each page independently.
- **Include Enhancements and Text:** To make your photos more engaging, include text:
  - ➢ **Text Panels:** You can add details, captions, and page names using the text panels. Modify the colors, fonts, and sizes to match your book's style.
- **Examine and Complete:** Prior to releasing:
  - ➢ **Preview:** Make sure everything is in its proper place by reviewing your book's layout in preview mode.
  - ➢ **Proofing:** Check for errors such as misspellings, improper spacing, and inconsistent designs.
- **Publish or Export:** As soon as you're joyful:
  - ➢ **Export Options:** To print your book yourself, you can save it as a PDF or JPEG file.
  - ➢ **Blurb Integration:** To send your design to a professional printer, click Send Book to Blurb if you select Blurb.

Making Custom Layouts and Print Templates

Photographers can create custom layouts and print templates in Adobe Lightroom Classic to create one-of-a-kind print arrangements that suit their needs. Without the need for additional software, this is particularly useful for creating layouts, contact sheets, or images that appear to have been printed by a professional printer. Open Lightroom Classic and select the Print Module to get started. All of the printing customization options and settings are located here. Selecting one of the three plan types—Single Image/Contact Sheet, Picture Package, or Custom Package—is the first step in the printing process. You have the greatest flexibility to arrange several images on a single page whatever you like with the Custom Package option. Once in the Print Module, select the page and print settings, along with the printer, paper size, and direction. Select "JPEG File" as the Print To option if you would rather to create a digital layout to export rather than print out. The layout will be saved as a high-quality image file as a result. To ensure that the prints are clear, set the file resolution to at least 300 PPI. The layout needs to be planned out next. This entails manually placing, resizing, and creatively arranging the images on the website. In Lightroom Classic, you may drag and drop images into the page from the filmstrip at the bottom. Either directly or through the Cells panel, which has preset sizes, you can enter custom measures. You may adjust the style and make sure it appears well by adjusting the cell orientation, spacing, and margins. You must save the template after finishing the design so you can utilize it later. Lightroom users can easily access their saved custom layouts via the Template Browser. After giving it a name and clicking the "+" button, the new template shows up under "User Templates," which makes it simple to use again for different print jobs. After you're satisfied with the plan, you can print the file or export it. Clicking "Print to file" saves the plan as an image that you may print or send online if you export as a JPEG file. Making sure the printer settings are correct before selecting "Print" will guarantee that the finished product is what was intended for those who print directly from Lightroom.

Exporting Pictures

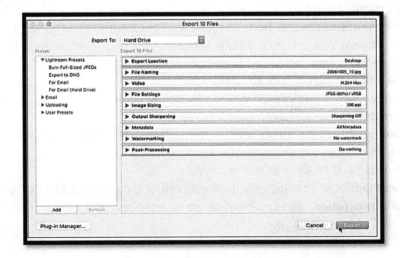

The following procedures will help you save images from Lightroom Classic to a computer, hard disk, or Flash drive:

- You may choose which images to send from the Grid view.
- You can either select File > Export or click the Export button in the Library module. Select Export To > Hard Drive if the Export box has a menu at the top.

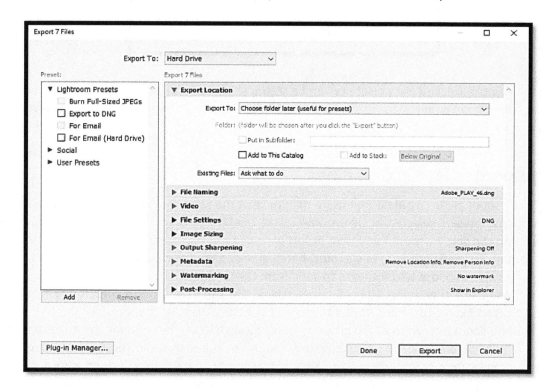

The number of shots that will be sent is indicated at the very top of the Export text box. You can select the type of file, alter file names, and perform other tasks with expanded panels. Select Export To > Hard Drive from the Export Location panel to save the file to a flash drive. Select Export To > Specific Folder after that. Next, locate the Flash drive by clicking Choose.

- If you'd like, you can select an export setting. Several presets in Lightroom Classic make it simple to save images as specific file types. For instance, Lightroom Classic's "For Email" choice instantly creates and delivers a 72-dpi JPEG image. If you select a setting from the list on the left side of the Export box, you can move directly to step 6.
- In the several Export dialog box panels, you can choose a target folder, name standards, and other options.

You can select a color space and style for the images you wish to transmit using the File Settings tab. Formats such as JPEG, PSD, TIFF, PNG, DNG, or the original are available for selection. The Image Sizing window allows you to select the image's dimensions and quality.

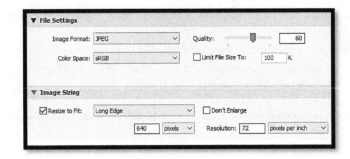

- If you'd like, you can preserve your file settings. On the left side of the Export text field is the Preset panel. From there, click the Add button. Your file selections will be saved so you can access them whenever you want.
- Click "Export."

Exporting in Multiple Batches

The same set of pictures can be sent more than once at the same time. When you share a photo with several presets selected in Lightroom Classic, one image is sent out for each option you select. You can select a format and then export your images if you would want to export them in that format. **To send your images via multi-batch export, take the following actions:**

- You may choose which images to send from the Grid view.
- You can either select File > Export or click the Export button in the Library module. Select Export To > Hard Drive if the Export box has a menu at the top.
- You can select which of the preset names you wish to use by checking the boxes next to them before uploading your own photos. All of the settings in the Export dialog box panels are disabled when you check a preset box. Click on the preset whose export settings you wish to view or modify, then uncheck all the boxes that are ticked.
  - Press "Batch Export."

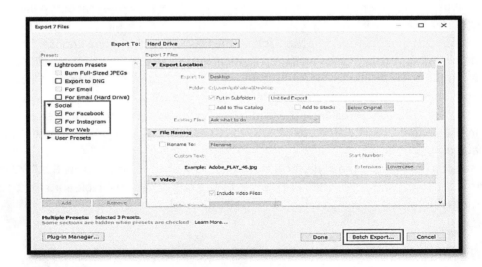

You are unable to select the Email and CD/DVD export settings because their boxes are not selected.

- One of the following actions should be taken in the Batch Export box:
  - ➤ If you haven't previously, choose a location for each setting individually.
  - ➤ To select the primary folder where all of the presets will be stored, click Choose Parent Folder. Any locations saved in a setup are lost once the parent folder is selected. Following this, each setup's Destination setting is modified to Put in Subfolder.
  - ➤ If you selected the presets in this box, you may also modify the Custom Text and Start Number settings that were established when the preset was created.
- Click "Export."

Reminder: In the event of a name conflict, the preset's name is appended to the end of the cloned file's name if multiple files share the same name.

Utilize Presets to Export Pictures

Using export presets allows you to send images to common locations easily. **You can transmit JPEG files that are suitable for sharing to friends or clients using one of Lightroom Classic's settings.**

- Picture exporting is simple. Simply select the ones you want, then select File > Export with Preset or click the Export button.
- Select a location. **The following export options are pre-configured in Lightroom Classic:**
  - ➤ **Burn Full-Sized JPEGs:** The images are converted to sRGB and tagged with the highest quality, without scaling, and at 240 pixels per inch before being sent. This option saves the files to the location you specify at the top of the Export dialog box for CD/DVD files by default. The files are stored in a folder called Lightroom Classic Burned Exports.
  - ➤ **Export to DNG:** Images are exported as DNG files. After you click Export, this setting doesn't tell you what to do, so you can choose the folder where the files will go.
  - ➤ **For Email:** Opens a message box where you may send the images and compose an email.
  - ➤ **For Email (Hard disk):** Stores images as sRGB JPEG files on your hard disk. The uploaded photos are not very excellent, have a resolution of 72 pixels per inch, and can only be 640 pixels width or height. After Lightroom Classic is finished, you can view the images in either the Finder (Mac OS) or the Explorer (Windows). Simply click "Export" and select the location for the file's storage.

Saving export configurations as presets

- Select the export options you wish to preserve in the Export box.
- The text box has a window labeled "Preset." Click "Add" at the bottom of that panel.
- Click Create when the New Preset box appears, then select Preset Name to give it a name.

Utilizing the Previous Configurations to Export Pictures

The parameters that were manually selected the previous time you exported can be used to export photos. This list contains modified presets.

When using export presets, you must perform this in order for the Export with Previous command to function.

- Select the images you want to send.
- Select File > Export with Previous from the menu. Getting your photographs out of Lightroom Classic requires a number of steps. **How to accomplish it:**
  - ➢ Start Lightroom Classic on your computer and make sure the collection of images you wish to send is visible.
  - ➢ Go to the Library module and select the pictures you wish to transmit. You can view many photos at once in the Grid view. You can enlarge one to see it more clearly in the Loupe view.
  - ➢ After choosing the images you wish to use, open the options by pressing Ctrl+Shift+E (Windows) or Cmd+Shift+E (Mac). From then on, choose File > Export.
  - ➢ Select the destination for the file's transmission by opening the Export window. On your computer, pick the folder you wish to save the photos you sent.
  - ➢ In "File Settings," you can select the color area, file size, and quality. TIFF and JPEG formats are widely used. Decide on the desired level of quality.
  - ➢ If necessary, you can adjust the size of your photographs under the Image Sizing section. If necessary, you might include a number or a unit of measurement.
  - ➢ Under "Metadata," you have the option to include metadata, such as copyright details. If you'd like, you can also remove location data.
  - ➢ Please watermark the images you share using the Watermarking tool. You can adjust the marking's settings to meet your needs.
  - ➢ By applying sharpening in the Output Sharpening section, you can improve the images' appearance both on paper and on the screen. Adjust the settings as necessary.
  - ➢ You can do more after exporting by visiting the Export window's additional sections, like Post-Processing. In this instance, Adobe Photoshop or another program may need to be used to open the images.
  - ➢ If you email photos frequently, save the settings you use most frequently as a default. You can then utilize them once again.
  - ➢ Click "Export" to transmit the file when all the options have been adjusted. As soon as the information is requested, Lightroom Classic will begin delivering the selected images to the specified address.
  - ➢ Select the Export Status tab in the Library module to view the current situation. Your photos will be in the folder you were provided after it's finished.

Branding and Watermarking Your Work

Step one: Bring in an image

Adding all of the images you wish to categorize to Lightroom is the first step. Click on any of the previews in the library module to add them if they have already been posted. A photograph should be edited, cropped, or resized before a watermark is applied.

Step two: Make a Watermark

Next, select the "Edit" module and slide the mouse pointer over it to bring up a drop-down menu with a lot of options. This menu has "Edit Watermarks" selected. You can add either a text watermark or a graphic watermark using the watermark editor window that will open as a result. Only one type can be added at a time, though, as enabling one will disable the options for the other type.

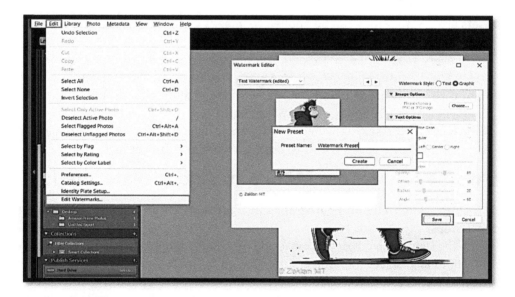

How Can a Text Watermark Be Made? You can label your photographs with your brand name or website name by following these steps:

+ To start, search for a drop-down menu in the upper left corner. Then select "Custom" from that option.
+ Locate and click the Text option for Watermark Style at the top of the Watermark editing window.
+ Next, enter your website address or brand name in the text field beneath the example.
+ Next, you can modify the text by selecting the font type, style, and layout under "Text Options." Afterward, you can view a preview of the image and amend the text.

- By selecting a fancy color and adding a shadow to the text, you can further alter your logo. To adjust the color, distance, radius, and angle of the shadow, uses the scroll bar.
- By clicking on the text and dragging its corner, you can manually adjust its size. However, make sure that the "Proportional" option is selected. If not, you can select "Fit" or "Fill" to instantly alter the marking's size.

How Can a Graphic Watermark Be Made? If you wish to use a name or image as a label, you must select "Graphic" under label Style. Next, select a JPG or PNG image from your computer. Make sure the background is clear to give it a more polished appearance. Using the various options in "Watermark Effects," you may alter the size and location of this watermark.

Step Three: Create Watermark Presets

Once your picture or word watermark is customized, click "Save" until a pop-up window displays. This window will appear. Click "Create."

Step 4: Watermark Several Pictures

Once presets are created, they can be applied to images of similar names. How to accomplish it:
- Select every image you wish to send. You can select every image at once by selecting the first image, then selecting every image while holding down the shift key.
- Right-click on any image to bring up a new window, then select "Export."
- After a little scrolling down, select "Watermark."
- After selecting the settings you created in the previous step, email out the images. This part of our website explains how to use Lightroom's export settings.

How to Use Lightroom Mobile to Add a Watermark

To apply a stamp when editing photographs in Lightroom on an iPhone or Android device, follow these steps:
- Open the Lightroom editor and make any necessary adjustments to the image.
- After finishing, select the "Share" icon located in the top right corner of the Lightroom mobile interface. This will open a new box with numerous options.
- To open a new window with additional features, scroll all the way to the bottom and select "Export as..." You must check the "Include Watermark" box in this window until it turns blue.
- Next, select "Customize." Text and Graphic are the two options at the top of the newly shown window. You can choose anybody you wish.
- Click on Text and enter your company name, brand name, or any other desired text to use it as a stamp.
- The following stage, Customize Text, is comparable to Lightroom Classic. This can be accomplished by adjusting the letter's size, style, color, position, density, horizontal offset, and vertical offset. Choose your preferred image, send the logo as a PNG file, and alter its size and positioning if you wish to use it as a watermark.

- After you're finished personalizing everything, click the checkmark in the top right corner and then the back button.
- A pop-up window with several sharing options will appear at the bottom of the screen. Photos can be shared on any platform or saved on your phone.

CHAPTER TEN

THE LIGHTROOM CLASSIC: ADVANCED COLOR GRADING

Principles of Grading and Color Theory

The study of color theory examines how colors interact, what they signify, and how to combine them to improve an object's appearance. It provides a methodical approach to learning about and utilizing color in art and design.

The Color Wheel

One of the most crucial tools in color theory is a color wheel, which shows the relationships between colors. It consists of:
- The three primary colors are yellow, blue, and red. You can't mix other colors to make these hues.
- Secondary Colors: created by combining two basic colors, they include green, orange, and purple.
- Red-orange and blue-green are examples of tertiary colors, which are blends of primary and secondary hues.

You can create color schemes that complement one another by arranging these colors in the correct sequence on the color wheel.

Harmony of Colors

Combining colors in a pleasing way is known as color balance. Typical plans include:
- **Complementary Colors:** Orange and blue, for example, are complementary colors since they are on different sides of the color wheel. Their looks are dynamic and highly diverse.
- On the color wheel, analogous colors are those that are adjacent to one another, such as blue, blue-green, and green. They create serene and soothing designs.
- **Triadic Colors:** These color schemes, such as red, yellow, and blue, have three colors evenly distributed throughout the color wheel.

Artists can select color schemes that convey the appropriate emotions and messages with the use of these harmonies.

Context and Perception of Color

Colors can appear differently depending on the context. In this instance, a gray square may appear cooler against a red background and warmer against a blue one. Since colors can alter the appearance of other colors and the overall perception of an arrangement, it is crucial for designers to understand how colors interact with one another.

Principles of Color Grading

Color grading is the process of altering and enhancing the colors of images, such as pictures and videos. Creating a particular look or feel is the aim. It is necessary to make both creative and technical adjustments.

Tones: Warm or Cool?

Warm tones (yellow, orange, and red) make you feel invigorated and warm, while cool tones (purple, green, and blue) make you feel serene and at ease. Selecting between warm and cool tones can significantly alter the audience's emotional response.

Saturation and Contrast

You may alter how bright and various colors appear by adjusting the contrast and brightness. Higher contrast and brightness can provide a dramatic and dynamic design, while lower settings might create a softer, more muted look. These adjustments help focus attention and establish the mood of the visual work.

Style and Consistency

A project's visual narrative will flow if the color grading is consistent throughout. Using a particular color scheme or design enhances the mood and aids in telling stories.

Real-World Use

When applying grading and color theory:
- **Recognize the Emotional Impact:** Select hues that correspond with the feelings you want to arouse.
- **Test and Modify:** Try out various color schemes and grading schemes to observe the results.
- **Get Feedback:** Find out what people think of your color choices by getting their thoughts.

Making Advanced Changes with the Color Grading Panel

Using Lightroom Classic's Color Grading tool, you may alter the hues of various areas of an image with varying tones. By making specific adjustments to the highlights, midtones, and shadows for hue, saturation, and brightness, you can alter the overall color scheme and mood of the image. Split Toning has been superseded as a tool by Color Grading in Lightroom Classic version 10.0. It provides a more precise method of selecting colors with color wheels and allows you to alter the midtones. Simply locate the Color Grading panel in the Develop module to begin using Color Grading. The adjustment mode above the panel can be changed. In conclusion, color grading allows you to adjust the toning both globally and individually. This provides you more control over the final product and improves the accuracy of color adjustments performed after the fact.

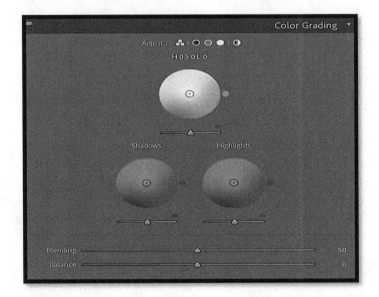

How to Use Lightroom's Global Color Grading

Simple color ranges may be changed more easily with Lightroom's Color Grading tool, which is essentially an improved version of Split Toning. Since there aren't many shadows in the image below, for instance, you can use Color Grading's global adjustment to make the image appear warmer. Drag the color wheels to find the color you want. **Fine modification is possible with the hue and saturation parameters below.**

The fact that the color wheels on the Color Grading panel eliminate the confusion that the hue slider created is among its better features. A purple-red color is on the right side of the red hue scale, while a yellowish-red color is on the left. The hues next to red on the color wheel are exactly what you see, albeit it can be challenging to interpret from the scale alone. Using color grading makes it much simpler to comprehend and adjust the hue setting. You only need to move the color wheel to make changes, and you can immediately see the results in the image on the left, making it quite simple to use.

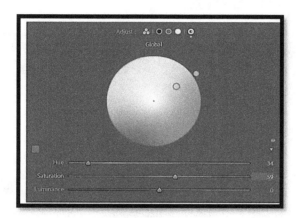

We will discuss each of the three really helpful Color Grading tools one at a time:

- **Sliders for HSL Adjustment:** On the right side of the Shadows, Midtones, Highlights, and Global panels are a tiny triangle icon. Clicking on it brings up the HSL parameter buttons. You can make adjustments to reduce the image's size in the Global panel without returning to the Basic settings for final adjustments. This increases the efficiency of color editing and repetitive tasks.

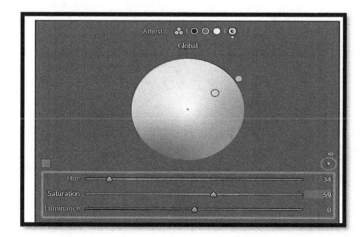

- **Personalized Colors:** You can select from a variety of Custom Colors using the tiny circles on the left side of the Shadows, Midtones, Highlights, and Global panels. These are comparable to Lightroom Classic's default settings and function nicely. However, the most helpful feature in Custom Colors is the eyedropper tool. To sample colors and adjust tone, move the eyedropper tool to any area of the image while depressing the mouse button. (Depending on the point you selected, Lightroom will automatically adjust the photo's brightness and hue.) This preserves the natural color grading results without adding colors that don't match, which would give the image an artificial or strange appearance. Using the colors that are already present in the image is the greatest method for selecting colors.

+ **Examining the Impact of Adjustment:** There is a tiny eye emblem on the right side of the Shadows, Midtones, Highlights, and Global panels. By doing this, you can observe how the colors appeared before and after the correction effects were turned off. (Holding it down permanently disables the effects; clicking it temporarily disables them; and releasing the mouse button restores the adjustment effects.) The finest part of this feature is that it is not saved in the past. As a result, viewing modification effects is quick and simple without interfering with editing.

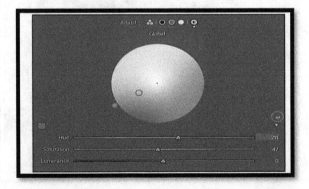

Color grading involves making one-by-one adjustments to a photograph's highlights, shadows, and midtones. You can choose between the various color grading styles using the buttons at the top of the Color Grading window. The 3-Way panel displays the color wheels for highlights, shadows, and midtones simultaneously. You may adjust the midtones, highlights, and shadows all in one location with the 3-way panel.

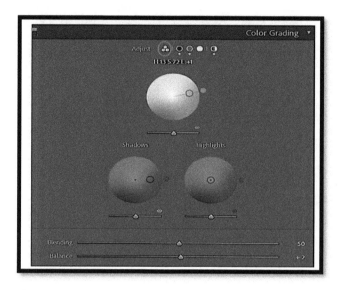

A brief overview of highlights, shadows, and midtones is provided here, along with instructions on how to adjust each tone independently depending on its effects:
- The brightest sections of the image, which are often white or almost white, are called highlights.
- The darkest sections of a photograph are called shadows, and they are typically black or nearly black regions captured in low light.
- The areas of an image that lie between the blacks and highlights are known as midtones. You can adjust the overall color and tones of the picture to make it appear smoother and more natural by adjusting the midtones.

Each panel has balancing and mixing buttons that function the same regardless of where they are positioned.

Blending Preferences

One way to think of the mixing setting is as the strength or transparency of the effect. It enables you to alter your three-tone adjustment to its desired impact. For instance, reducing the blending option will lessen the overall impression if you feel the colors are too intense and artificial. Raising it will intensify the effect if you're not online.

Adjusting the balance

The balancing option alters the range of how many the highlights and shadows influence one another. By altering the balance, you can alter the original image's color appearance. For instance, if an image has a lot of shadows and you want the warm tones of the highlights to cover a larger area and give the shadows some warmth, you can adjust the balancing scale. This function also allows the shadow color to alter the bright spots and middle tones.

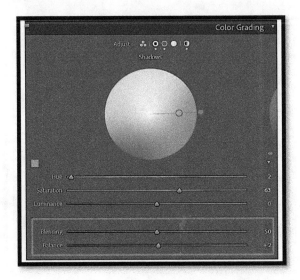

How to Make the Most of Lightroom Color Grading

Even better results can be achieved by combining global adjustments with highlights, shadows, and midtone tweaks using Lightroom Classic's Color Grading function. Following a specific order can be useful when color grading. Examine your photo's tones first. If the arrangement is clear and the tones are fairly straightforward, you can employ global direct modifications. For more complex effects, such as city streets or sunsets with buildings, you can first adjust the highlights, shadows, and midtones individually in the 3-Way panel to obtain a general sense of the look you desire. Then proceed to adjust each tone independently. Finally, consider whether you want to add a new hue to the shot using global changes. There are no universally applicable principles or approaches when it comes to color grading; it's a personal process. Nonetheless, there is a creative tool that can speed up and simplify color grading.

Tone Curve for Accurate Color Management

Because the sliders in the Basic panel accomplish the same task in a different manner, it is simple to overlook the Tone Curve panel in Lightroom Classic. Lightroom Classic can be used without ever opening the Tone Curve tab. It's helpful to know how to utilize the Tone Curve panel because it contains some tools that the Basic panel does not.

- You can target particular tones in your photo with the Targeted Adjustment Tool (TAT). The Basic panel does not allow this.
- To change color values, you can modify the Red, Green, and Blue Channel Curves.
- Using the other tools in Lightroom Classic, you can't achieve a matte finish.

↓ The Point Curve can be inverted, which is helpful for scanning negatives.

The tone curve: what is it?

The Tone Curve is a vertical line that displays the tones in your image, ranging from darkest (bottom left) to brightest (top right). Lightroom Classic has five tone curves. The Point Curve, Red Channel Curve, Green Channel Curve, and Blue Channel Curve are their names. In Lightroom Classic, each Tone Curve is displayed on a graph. A graph known as a histogram displays the color or tone values in your image on X and Y axes that range from 0 to 255. Avoid this histogram as it is not the same as the one in the Histogram panel. The Parametric and Point Curves can be used to lighten or darken certain tones in your image. Additionally, they can be used to adjust the brightness. The color channel curves allow you to alter color values but not tone values.

Tone Curve Panel

This image displays the Point Curve (right) and the Parametric Curve (left) in the Tone Curve panel.

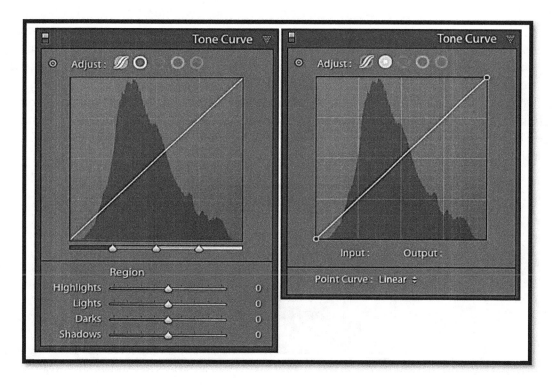

This image displays the three-color channel curves.

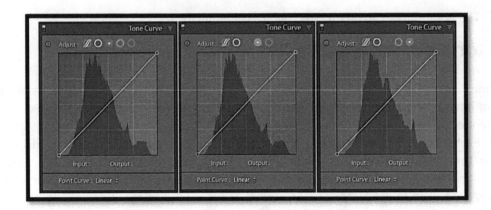

All of the curves appear to be in their default, or normal, states. When the curve is a straight line, the colors and tones remain unchanged.

Including Control Points

Despite the fact that each curve performs a distinct function, they all function similarly. The Tone Curve's form can be altered by adding or moving a few control points. This alters the image's colors or tones. Each Tone Curve has two control points: one at the bottom left and one at the top right. When you drag the curve to a new location, it moves with the control point. Click on the line that crosses the screen to see additional control points. By adding and altering control points, the curve transforms from a straight line to a curve. Adding more control points will give you more control over the curve's shape. The Point Curve with its two initial control points is shown on the left. Three additional control points are on the right, and one new control point is in the center. The control point that is being moved or was moved last is the white one. The ones that have already been moved are the black control points.

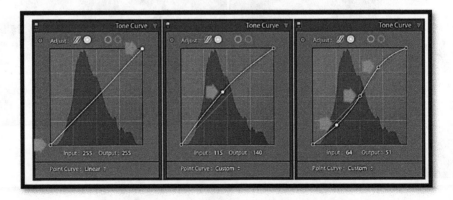

Additionally, the input and output variables indicate the location of the current control point on the curve. The current control point can be moved by clicking on the input or output value and entering a new value.

Using the Point Curve

Click the gray circle at the top of the Tone Curve window to activate the Point Curve. Click in the center of the Point Curve to add a control point. Drag the Control Point up to lighten the image (bottom left). Drag it down to make it darker (below center). The contrast will also be increased by adding two more control points to create a S curve (below right).

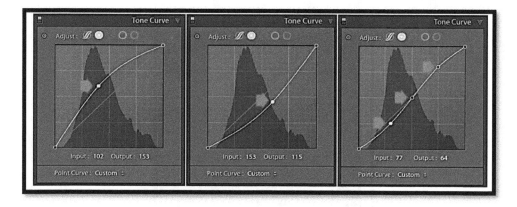

Utilizing the Parametric Curve

Clicking the Curve button at the top of the Tone Curve window will bring up the Parametric Curve. If you have already adjusted the Point Curve, the Parametric Curve retains its shape but lacks control points. Use the buttons at the bottom to adjust the tone. When you move a tool, the line indicates which area of the Tone Curve changes. Below, you can see the regions where the buttons for Highlights, Lights, and Darks vary.

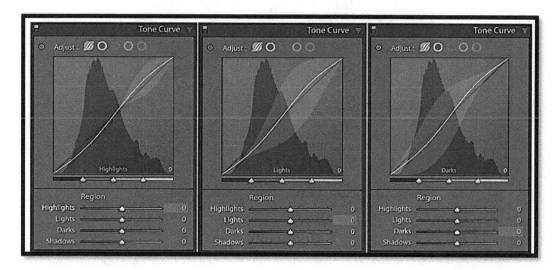

The Tool for Targeted Adjustment (TAT)

The Basic panel allows you to do anything you want. So far, we have learnt how the Tone Curve functions. However, the Tone Curve panel offers more tools than the Basic panel, as we have already seen. The first is the Targeted Adjustment Tool (TAT).

When using a parametric curve or a point curve with the Targeted Adjustment Tool, you can:

- Click on the icon for the Targeted Adjustment Tool, which is indicated below.

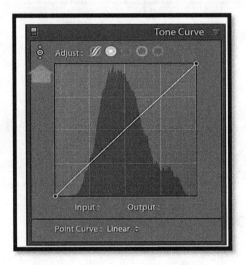

- Position the pointer over the image. To indicate the value of the tones beneath the cursor, Lightroom adds a control point to the Tone Curve.

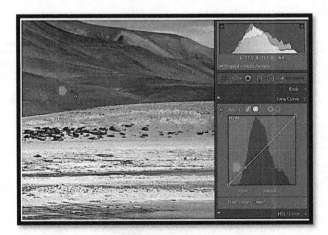

- Click on the image to add a control point to the Tone Curve. Holding down the button allows you to move the mouse up or down. The control point is moved up and down. Alternatively, you might shift the arrow on the Tone Curve by releasing the mouse button.

✛ You can increase the number of control points in the Tone Curve in this way.
Because it allows you to select the precise tones you wish to alter, the Targeted Adjustment Tool is useful.

Utilizing the Tone Curves for Color Channels

While the Red, Green, and Blue Channel Curves all function similarly, altering the curve's shape alters the colors rather than the tones. For instance, moving the Blue Channel Curve up makes the colors in the image bluer.

As you move the Blue Channel Curve downward, things become more yellow.

Use the Red Channel Curve to turn colors red or green. Use the Green Channel Curve to turn colors green or pink. **Reminder:** Adobe added colors to the screen to show you how the colors changed when the layout was altered in Lightroom Classic 9.3 (see below).

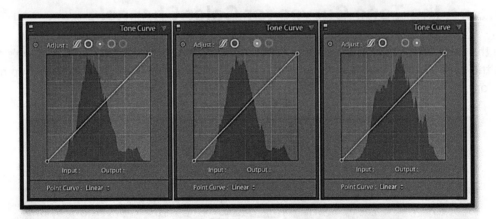

Use the Targeted Adjustment Tool for even more accuracy. For example, a Blue Channel Curve like the one below adds blueness to the shadows without significantly altering the colors. The soft effect may appeal to you and be helpful for outdoor or portrait photography.

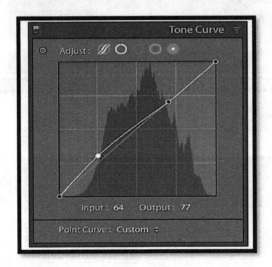

Cool color effects, such as those seen in Develop Presets, can also be added with them.

How to Make a Matte Effect

The Tone Curve can be used to create the illusion that a photograph was taken on film with the matte effect or written on matte paper. The implication is that the darkest shadows are gray, not black.

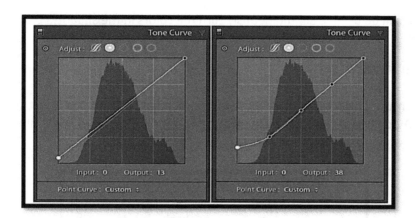

The matte effect is created by the two Point Curves below. The more you raise the left control point, the better it functions.

It performs admirably in black-and-white images.

This technique can be used to simultaneously turn the colors in the shadows blue using the Blue Channel Curve. It frequently occurs in fashion and images.

The Curve inversion

Finally, you can use scanning or other digitization techniques to turn a negative image into a positive one. A point curve that has been inverted is this one. To move the control points at the ends of the curve, simply click and drag them.

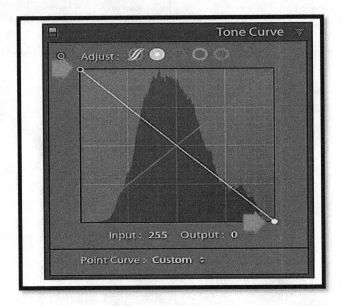

It affects your scanned negative in this way.

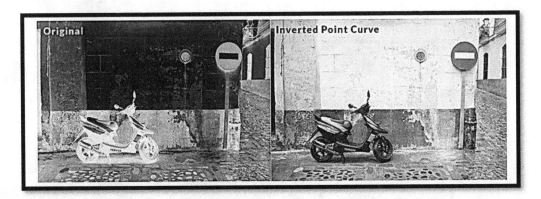

You should now have a better understanding of Lightroom Classic's Tone Curve panel and some of its features thanks to this course. Although not all shooters need to use it, it does include some helpful tools that you can employ if necessary.

CHAPTER ELEVEN

LINKING LIGHTROOM TO OTHER APPS IN THE ADOBE CREATIVE CLOUD

Using Adobe Bridge with Lightroom

Adobe Lightroom Classic and Adobe Bridge are two powerful applications in the Adobe Creative Cloud package. Photographers and other creative professionals can utilize each of its unique qualities. Adobe Bridge is a versatile file reader that makes it simple to access and arrange a variety of media files, whereas Lightroom Classic is renowned for its strong organizing and editing capabilities. You can make your work easier by combining these two programs, but only if you understand their distinct capabilities and know how to utilize them properly.

Comprehending Adobe Lightroom Classic and Bridge

Users may effortlessly navigate between files and directories with Adobe Bridge, which functions as a robust file browser. It displays accurate thumbnails and information for a wide variety of file kinds, including RAW images, PSDs, PDFs, and videos. Bridge is therefore excellent for arranging and reviewing files prior to importing them into other Adobe applications. In contrast, Lightroom Classic is a catalog-based system that enables photographers to add, arrange, edit, and share images from a single central database. With its sophisticated editing features, keyword tagging, and collection management, it may be utilized for all facets of photo administration and post-processing.

How to Include Bridge in Your Lightroom Classic Process

Despite Lightroom Classic's abundance of photo organization options, there are situations in which Bridge might be useful:

- **Initial File Review and Culling:** Before importing your photos into Lightroom Classic, you may quickly browse through and remove any unnecessary ones in Bridge. Bridge eliminates the need to import photos by allowing you to view them straight from your storage devices. This speeds up the selection process. After you've located the images you want to work with, you can edit them further in Lightroom Classic.
- **Managing Non-Photographic Assets:** Bridge serves as a hub for creative professionals that handle many media formats, such as documents, graphics, and videos, to organize and access these files. Bridge can facilitate your workflow by managing assets that don't fit in Lightroom's catalog because it can handle a wider variety of file types than Lightroom Classic.
- **Editing information and Batch Renaming:** Bridge offers strong capabilities for editing information and batch renaming. Before importing your files into Lightroom Classic, you

can give them consistent names and details. This guarantees that the catalog is simplified and well-organized from the beginning.

The Best Ways to Combine Lightroom Classic with Bridge

The following best practices should be kept in mind while integrating Bridge with Lightroom Classic to ensure a seamless and error-free workflow:

- **Don't Move or Rename Files Outside of Lightroom Classic:** You should only move or rename files inside Lightroom Classic after you've loaded them. You risk having broken links and missing files in your library if you perform these actions outside of Lightroom, such as using Bridge or your operating system's file browser.
- **Use Bridge for Pre-Import chores:** Bridge can be used for pre-import chores such as initial culling, group renaming, and metadata application before files are brought into Lightroom Classic. By doing this, you can maintain the organization of your Lightroom catalog and ensure that all of your files are immediately accessible.
- **Pay Attention to Metadata Synchronization:** After importing files into Lightroom Classic, you may make changes to the metadata in Bridge, which may not immediately appear in Lightroom. The "Read Metadata from Files" feature in Lightroom Classic can be used to add the most recent data to the library and exchange metadata.

Lightroom and Adobe Stock Synchronization

By sending images straight from their library to the stock website, photographers may expedite their work when they link Adobe Lightroom Classic to Adobe Stock. This combination facilitates handling and submitting your photography work by making it simpler to post high-quality images to Adobe Stock.

Adding Pictures to Adobe Stock from Lightroom Classic

Use these procedures to upload your Lightroom Classic images to Adobe Stock:

- Open Lightroom Classic, and then select the Library module to access it.
- **Locate the Adobe Stock Publish Service:** Look for the Adobe Stock option in the Publish Services box on the left. You might need to add Adobe Stock as a new publishing service by clicking the "+" button if it's not visible.
- **Verify Your Adobe ID:** Make sure the Adobe ID linked to your Adobe Stock contributor account is the one you are using to log in. For the integration to work properly, this is essential.
- **Get Your Pictures Ready:** Choose the pictures you want to upload. Before moving on, it is important to edit and finalize all adjustments.
- Use the Adobe Stock Collection by dragging and dropping: In the Publish Services tab, drag the chosen photos into the Adobe Stock collection.
- **Add Metadata and Keywords:** Enter pertinent titles, descriptions, and keywords for every image. Your photographs' discoverability on Adobe Stock is improved by this metadata.

- **Publish the Images:** To start the upload procedure, click the "Publish" button. The photos will be moved to your Adobe Stock contributor account via Lightroom Classic.
- **Complete work on Adobe Stock Contributor Portal:** Once your work has been uploaded, go to the Adobe Stock Contributor portal to check it. You can add more metadata, make last-minute changes, and submit your photos for approval here.

Integration of Adobe Fonts and Lightroom

Enhancing the writing in your work is simple when you add Adobe Fonts to Lightroom Classic, particularly when creating photo books, slideshows, or watermarks. Adobe Fonts is part of your Creative Cloud subscription. This provides you with access to a vast font collection that may be used in Lightroom Classic and other Adobe products. This makes it simple to maintain the same design for your projects. Before using Adobe Fonts in Lightroom Classic, you must enable them in the Creative Cloud Desktop application. To access the Fonts section, launch the Creative Cloud application on your PC. You can look through a huge selection of typefaces designed for both personal and professional use here. Once you've found a font that suits your needs, click "Activate" to make it instantly accessible in all Adobe applications, including Lightroom Classic. These fonts should appear in Lightroom Classic's font list when you launch the application because they were loaded straight onto your computer. If the newly enabled fonts do not appear, Lightroom Classic may need to be restarted in order to refresh its font collection.

Once activated, the styles can be utilized in various Lightroom Classic sections. For instance, the new typefaces will be available in the text style options when creating a picture book in the Book Module. This gives you more options for font customisation, which helps you align your picture book's look with your creative idea. Similarly, you may use the Watermark Editor to create your own custom text-based watermarks using these designs. Choosing a font is made easier with Adobe Fonts, allowing you to add a subtle brand mark or a more visible signature-style layer to your images. Because Lightroom Classic relies on fonts that are already installed on your computer, any font you add or activate using Adobe Fonts ought to function in the program. Here are some solutions to try if you're having issues with the enabled fonts not showing up. Restarting Lightroom Classic is usually the simplest solution to the issue. This causes the application to reexamine its font list and identify any recently loaded fonts. Verify that the typefaces are correctly enabled in the Creative Cloud application if it doesn't resolve the issue. Occasionally, a fleeting sync error may prevent the fonts from appearing. Turning the font off and back on again can resolve the problem if this occurs. It's also known that on certain operating systems, particularly macOS, Lightroom Classic occasionally has issues identifying fonts. Making ensuring that Lightroom Classic and your operating system are both up to date might help prevent compatibility issues if fonts aren't appearing the way you want them to. If you continue to experience issues, Adobe's support page and community forums offer additional details and solutions from other users who have experienced similar issues. You should properly integrate Adobe Fonts with Lightroom Classic to improve the appearance of your work. Whether you are creating text overlays, adding fashionable watermarks, or designing a picture book that will be professionally produced, having access to high-quality typefaces helps ensure that your work looks polished and well-put together.

Combining Adobe Premiere Pro and Lightroom for Video Editing

If you wish to utilize the same color settings for both photographs and films, adding Adobe Lightroom to Adobe Premiere Pro can greatly simplify the video editing process. Lightroom has few tools for video editing and is mostly used for photo processing. Conversely, Premiere Pro is a robust video editing program that enables sophisticated color correction and grading. You can make your work appear to be cohesive by utilizing the greatest capabilities of both apps.

Recognizing Lightroom and Premiere Pro's Potential

Adobe Lightroom provides a number of basic video editing tasks, including clip trimming and basic color adjustments. But compared to its picture editing tools, it is less useful in this area. For more complex tasks like merging numerous clips, making transitions, and doing intricate color grading, Adobe advises using a product designed specifically for video editing, such as Premiere Pro.

Using Lightroom Presets with Premiere Pro to Edit Videos

One technique to maintain consistency across all of your media is to apply Lightroom presets to your films in Premiere Pro. Lightroom presets, particularly Look-Up Tables (LUTs), are converted into a file that Premiere Pro can read in this stage. **What you can do is this:**
- **Create or Choose a Lightroom Preset:** Lightroom allows you to create or choose a preset that specifies the color adjustments you desire.
- **Export the Preset as a LUT:** Use a third-party program, like a free LUT maker, to convert the Lightroom preset into a.cube file that can be utilized with Premiere Pro's Lumetri Color panel.
- **Open Premiere Pro and import the LUT:** Click the "Creative" tab in the Lumetri Color panel, then select "Browse" under "Look" to add the.cube file. This will add the LUT to Premiere Pro.
- **Apply the LUT to Your Video Clips:** After importing the LUT, you may apply it to your video clips to ensure that the color grading matches the Lightroom style you specified.

Organizing Media in Premiere Pro and Lightroom

Being able to manage your files effectively is crucial when alternating between Lightroom and Premiere Pro. Although Lightroom has some basic capabilities for organizing and editing films, it may not be compatible with all of the video types required for complete editing in Premiere Pro. For this reason, the best way to arrange and load your media files is to use Premiere Pro's Media

Browser. This technique ensures that every kind of video is recognized and handled appropriately during editing.

The Best Methods for a Smooth Workflow

When combining Lightroom and Premiere Pro, follow these tips to maximize your workflow:

- **Consistent Color Profiles:** Ensure that both tools are configured to use the same color profiles in order to maintain the color fidelity of your media.
- **Centralized Media Storage:** Store your media files in a single location accessible by Lightroom and Premiere Pro. This technique expedites the writing process and reduces file management issues.
- **Frequent Software Updates:** To take advantage of improved features and compatibility, make sure Lightroom and Premiere Pro are always running the most recent versions.

You can leverage the best features of both Lightroom and Premiere Pro to make your video editing process more effective and seamless if you know what each tool can accomplish and follow these integration guidelines.

CHAPTER TWELVE

UNDERSTANDING TIPS, TRICKS, AND
TECHNIQUES FOR TIME-SAVING

The Secret Tricks

No matter how much you know about Lightroom Classic, there always seems to be more to discover. Lightroom Classic is considerably more helpful and easy to use once you discover its secret tricks. I therefore thought it would be entertaining to compile a brief list of some tips that you should know but are probably unaware of. Let's discover their nature.

First Hidden Lightroom Classic Trick: Lengthen the Develop module sliders

Were you aware that the panels on the right may be widened by pulling them out? The benefit is that it makes the Develop module's sliders wider, enabling more precise manipulation. To view the icon below, move the mouse pointer above the left edge of the panels on the right. Then, move the mouse to the left by pressing and holding the left mouse button.

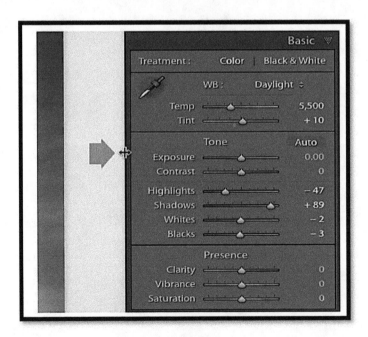

Here, you can see how the larger width (on the right) differs from the standard width (on the left). This is particularly useful on larger TVs and also works the other way around with the left-hand panels.

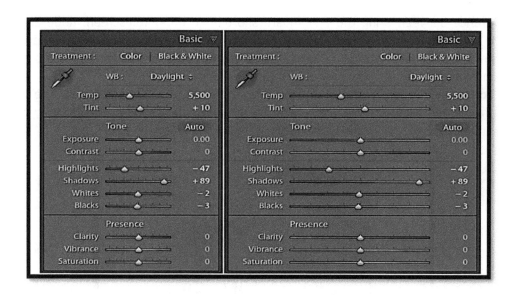

To make the panels on the right even larger on a Mac, click and drag while holding down the Alt key. Only the Develop module will be able to use this method.

Second Hidden Lightroom Classic Trick: Use Caps Lock to Enable Auto Advance

The simplicity of viewing and editing your photos is one of Lightroom Classic's strongest features. When I say "edit," I mean selecting which images to preserve and processing them in the Develop section. This is not difficult to accomplish if you are a landscape photographer who uses long exposures and captures fewer than 10 photos during a shoot. In this instance, selecting the best photos doesn't require much assistance. However, suppose you work as a wedding photographer and capture a large number of images at a single event. Assist this photographer! The greatest method for rapidly going through a large number of photographs is Auto Advance. Select Photo > Auto Advance to activate it. It's even faster if you use a computer button. To activate or deactivate Auto Advance, simply hit the Caps Lock key. Most computers feature a light that illuminates when Caps Lock is used, making it simple to quickly determine whether Auto Advance is enabled.

The difference between using the F keyboard shortcut to enter full-screen mode and the E keyboard shortcut to enter Loupe View is displayed below. Pressing nearly any key causes Lightroom Classic to automatically advance to the next shot. The Space bar is a significant exception. Instead, it zooms in and out of the current image.

- **Loupe View:** You can arrange a screen with the Filmstrip at the bottom and the image in the center, as seen below. The side panels will have to be concealed by you. This enables you to see the picture's place within the sequence.

- **Full screen:** The current photo and nothing else are shown on full screen. It provides you with the optimal view of your photos (see below).

Auto Advance can be used in a variety of ways.

- To select a flagged image, click the right button to proceed to the next one, or hit P to mark the image as a pick or X to indicate it as a reject.
- Hit 1, 2, 3, 4, or 5 to assign a star rating, hit 0 to delete one, or use the right arrow key to view the next image if you utilize star ratings.

Press F or Esc to exit full-screen view when you're finished.

The Third Hidden Lightroom Classic Trick: Rotate the Crop Overlay

When you wish to crop a landscape image to a portrait, you know how annoying it is to try to shift the Crop Overlay. Press the R key to rapidly access the Crop Overlay. There doesn't appear to be a straightforward method to alter Lightroom Classic's automatic rotation to match the angle of the image. Press X to accomplish that.

Below: Lightroom Classic sets the Crop Overlay's size and orientation to match the original image by default.

Below: To create an extreme crop and rotate the Crop Overlay, press X.

Fourth Hidden Lightroom Classic Tip: Resize the Spot Elimination Tool

Lightroom Classic's ability to predict which section of the image should be sampled in order to heal the selected area is not as strong as you may imagine. This annoys you when you open the Spot Removal Tool using the Q key shortcut. You can click to move the selected area to a different section of the image if you're unhappy with the result. However, did you know that you may use the backslash (/) key to instruct Lightroom Classic to select a different location for sampling? Until you achieve the desired effect, you can repeat it as often as you like. In this instance, the bright blob in the backdrop (represented by the circles below) is unnecessary; therefore I wanted to remove it.

Lightroom Classic's initial guess was incorrect.

However, the second one is far superior.

Fifth Hidden Lightroom Classic Trick: Automatic White and Black Points

There are some hidden Lightroom Classic techniques here that you may not be aware of. The first is that if you double-click on the text in the Basic panel rather than the Whites and Blacks sliders, Lightroom Classic will reset them to zero. This convenient feature makes it quick and simple to reset sliders. It also works with the majority of sliders in the Basic panel. Here is the second hidden trick. Lightroom Classic determines the optimal settings if you double-click the sliders while holding down the Shift key. It determines where to position both sliders so that there are no spaces between the histogram's left (shadows) and right (highlights) sections of the graph. Most photos immediately seem better following this easy modification. This technique is most effective when using the Whites and Blacks sliders to rapidly identify the image's white and black points. It is also compatible with the Basic Panel's other sliders.

Below: Holding down the Shift key, double-click the Whites and Blacks sliders. Be careful to double-click the text rather than the slider. Lightroom Classic believes this to be the ideal option if the slider remains at zero.

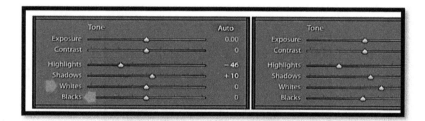

Sixth Hidden Lightroom Classic Trick: Flip a Graduated Filter

Did you know that a Graduated Filter may be flipped with the apostrophe key? Why you would want to flip a Graduated Filter may be on your mind. Allow me to demonstrate how this functions in the real world.

- Apply a graduated filter on the sky in a scene photo. Holding down the Shift key in Lightroom Classic will maintain the Graduated Filter in its proper position. To darken the sky, move the Highlights slider to the left. The Exposure slider will sometimes function better.

- To create a new Graduated Filter with the same parameters as the last one, pick up the pin for the Graduated Filter, right-click on it, and select "Duplicate."

- Pressing the shift key will flip the Graduated Filter. The background is now set to a lower Exposure. Double-click the Highlights slider to return it to 0 because it appears that you do not want the center to become darker. This new Graduated Filter can now be used to improve the center.

- Move the Clarity tool to the right to highlight the detail in the middle. You might also need to shift the Shadows tool to the right if this makes the center too dark.

In the end, you have applied two Graduated Filters—one to the ground and one to the sky. The difference between the before and after photos is evident.

The seventh hidden Lightroom classic trick: Resize the Spot Removal tool brush.

The Spot Removal tool can also be used in this manner. You probably already know that you can adjust the Spot Removal tool brush's size by using the '[' and ']' computer keys. The scroll wheel of a mouse can also be used. However, did you know that you may quickly adjust the brush's size? On a Mac, you can click and drag to adjust the brush size to your desired size while simultaneously holding down the Option and Command buttons. The ideal size is somewhat larger than the area that need repair. On a Windows computer, press and hold the Alt and Control keys.

The Eighth Hidden Lightroom Classic Trick: Using the Print module to format text

You can assemble a collection of images and add text to them using the Print module. You may, for instance, place a title beneath the pictures. However, the ID Plate is the only way to do it. In the Identity Plate Editor, you can input a few phrases and select the font type and size, but you can't alter elements that graphic professionals adore, such as kerning and leading. If you enjoy good fonts and styles, this is at least unpleasant. This hidden trick makes it simple to do that. Launch any text editor and enter the content you wish to include in your print. The editor has built-in capabilities for tracking (the space between letters) and other font quirks. To access the font options in Photoshop, open the Character panel. You can also utilize the type tools in InDesign if you have it. When you're finished, copy the text and enter it in the Identity Plate Editor's text field in Lightroom Classic. The text will remain in the style you choose when you click OK. The images below illustrate the change. The first one displays the type that Identity Plate used, and the second one utilizes type that I created using TextEdit, the built-in text editor on my Mac.

Finding the tips and techniques is difficult, but it's not that they're hidden. But if you know how to use them, Lightroom Classic is considerably faster and easier.

Using Personalized Presets

In essence, Lightroom Classic presets are a group of previously saved edit settings. Instead of making the same adjustments by hand for every image, you can rapidly apply your unique style. In addition to expediting your work, this technique ensures consistency throughout a shot or your entire portfolio, which is crucial for establishing a unified aesthetic. Consider the hectic schedule of a wedding photographer, who must ensure that hundreds of images portray a cohesive story. A good start is provided by presets, which can help you get 30% of the desired final look. After that, you can adjust things like cropping, exposure, white balance, and other particular adjustments. They help you do more while preserving your creative vision. Pro Tip: Consider presets as starting points. Even the most meticulously planned scene may require some adjusting to accommodate variations in lighting, subject matter, or design. Make any necessary improvements to each image by applying your critical eye.

Making Personalized Lightroom Classic Presets

In Lightroom Classic, creating your own presets is simple. You can create a theme that complements your editing style and works for a variety of projects by following these steps.

- **Perfectly Edit a Photo:** Start by locating an image that exemplifies the look you wish to get. The Develop module allows you to make changes to the exposure, contrast, color grading, tone curve, sharpening, noise reduction, and other settings until you are satisfied with the outcome.

- **Launch the Create Preset Dialog box:** To access the preset creation tool, click the "+" button in the Presets panel on the left and select "Create Preset..." This will open the New Develop Preset dialog box where you may configure your preset parameters.
- **Select Settings and Give Your Preset a Name:** The window contains options for various modifications, including Basic Tone, Color Grading, Detail, and more.
  - ➤ Give your preset a meaningful moniker, such "Soft Warm Portrait" or "Moody B&W Signature."
  - ➤ Choose a Preset Group: To make presets easier to find, arrange them into folders.
  - ➤ **Decide Which Configurations to Add:**
    - Think about removing parameters like Exposure or White Balance that can require special adjustments for each picture.
    - Incorporate the artistic alterations that characterize your style, such as tone curves, split tones, HSL modifications, and sharpening. After making your selection, click "Create" to save the configuration. It will appear in the group you selected's Presets panel.
- **Use Your New Preset on Additional Pictures:** To utilize your new option, select another image (or multiple images in batch mode) and click on it in the Presets panel. Right away, Lightroom will use the modifications you saved. The preset will be applied to any image you select in Grid or Filmstrip view. Because of this, it's ideal for editing multiple photos at once. After utilizing the preset, go over each image. To get it exactly right, the edit may require a few minor adjustments, such as a slight increase in shadow or exposure.
- **Improve and Revise Your Preset:** As you use it more, you could discover that you need to adjust a few settings. After you apply the preset to an image and make the required changes, right-click on the preset's name and select "Update with Current Settings." Your preset will now incorporate your most recent modifications if you confirm which settings you wish to update. You can now use your personalized Lightroom Classic setting! Well done! In the sections that follow, we'll discuss how to use presets efficiently and incorporate them into your workflow.

Expert Advice on Making the Most of Presets

Preset setup is just the first step. Knowing when and how to use them effectively will yield the finest outcomes.

- **Start with Presets:** While presets can serve as a starting point, you should always examine each image to see how it turned out. To ensure that each image is unique, adjust details like exposure or other adjustments by zooming in.
- Organize your collection by category, such as Portrait Presets, Landscape Presets, Black & White Looks, Matte Looks, and so forth, as your collection expands. When you require a preset, use explicit name standards to locate it fast.

- **There is no one-size-fits-all solution:** Be aware that a scene designed for a photo in the sun might not be suitable for a nighttime cityscape. If the default settings don't fit with your starting point, don't be scared to switch presets. Continue adjusting for various styles or lighting conditions.
- **Handle bulk Editing Carefully:** Although presets are excellent for bulk editing, you should always see the updated batch before proceeding. You might need to make your own adjustments if certain photos have lighting or color variations that a one-click preset cannot correct.
- **Manually Modify Preset Intensity:** Although Lightroom Classic has an integrated "preset strength" function, you can manually modify the intensity of the settings. After utilizing a preset, you can adjust the settings if it adds too much color or contrast.
- **Make a Favorites Collection:** Pick the presets that best capture your distinct style and that you use most frequently. After that, place them in an accessible folder. This expedites the writing process and makes your brand stand out.

Effective Strategies for Managing Large Image Libraries

To keep their work organized and get to it fast, digital artists and photographers need to understand how to effectively handle big-picture libraries. A suite of features included with Adobe Lightroom Classic facilitates finding and organizing photographs in sizable collections. **The following are some strategies for simplifying the management of large-picture libraries:**
- **Create a Uniform Folder Structure:** Make sure your storage device's folders are in order before importing photographs into Lightroom. This organization should make sense and fit your working style. You may arrange by event, employment, or year, for instance. Finding particular images when you need them is made simpler with a consistent folder structure.
- **Make Effective Use of Lightroom Catalogs:** A catalog system is used in Lightroom Classic to manage and modify picture information. Although a single catalog can accommodate many images, you may want to divide your work into multiple catalogs if you have numerous clients or projects. By keeping unneeded labor separate, this approach can help people perform their jobs more effectively and focus on specific tasks more easily.
- **Put keywords and metadata into practice:** Finding and filtering your images is made much simpler if you provide descriptive keywords and information either during or shortly after the import process. To create a robust database that can be promptly retrieved based on specific criteria, including elements like topic, location, and customer names.
- **Make Use of Collections and Intelligent Collections:** Lightroom's collections allow you to organize photos without having to move them around on your storage device. You can manually assemble images for projects or themes using standard collections. Smart Collections automatically compile images depending on pre-established record dates, ratings, or keywords. In addition to saving time, this maintains dynamic organization.
- **Use color labels, ratings, and flags:** Establish a regular procedure for grouping your photos according to editing status, quality, or other individual criteria. Signs, stars, and

color labels could be used. For instance, you may use color names to indicate the various stages of your editing process, flags to indicate which files have been chosen, and stars to indicate quality. This method facilitates accurate picture sorting and filtering.

- **Frequently Filter and Eliminate Superfluous Pictures:** Go through your collections from time to time to identify and eliminate duplicate or low-quality images. This maintains your catalog clean and conserves storage space, making it easier to manage and navigate. Establishing a routine culling procedure ensures that your library contains just your greatest work.

- **Optimize Catalog Settings and Previews:** Lightroom's speed can be significantly impacted by changing the viewing settings, particularly when dealing with huge files. You can save space on your hard disk and speed up your computer by creating standard-sized previews rather than full-size ones. Maintaining your catalog's functionality and security also involves creating regular copies of it and making use of Lightroom's built-in capabilities to enhance it.

- **Make Use of External Storage Options:** As your photo collection expands, you may wish to employ network-attached storage (NAS) devices or portable hard drives to store older or less-used images. You can easily manage photographs on many storage systems with Lightroom. This maintains the clarity and efficiency of your main drive.

- **Regular File Naming Practices:** Establish a common file naming convention during the import process to maintain organization and facilitate locating. Incorporating a date, event, or client name into a file's name helps improve organization and help users immediately comprehend what the file is.

CHAPTER THIRTEEN
DEBUGGING AND ASSISTANCE

Typical Lightroom Problems and Solutions

With its robust photo editing and organization features, Adobe Lightroom Classic is a comprehensive product for photographers. But occasionally, users could encounter issues that prevent them from operating as efficiently as they usually would. Your experience with the software can be much improved by being aware of these typical problems and how to resolve them.

Problems with Performance: Laggardness and Slowness

Many users complain that Lightroom Classic becomes sluggish over time, becoming slow to start up, slow to edit photographs, and slow to respond when switching between modules. Numerous factors, including large catalog files, insufficient system resources, or outdated graphics drivers, can contribute to these speed issues. You should constantly enhance your collection to address these problems. To accomplish this, select File > Optimize Catalog. This will improve the catalog's functionality by organizing the information. You can potentially speed up operations by increasing the size of the Camera Raw file. This option is located in Edit > Preferences > Performance. It allows you to increase the amount of space that picture data can be cached, which speeds up download. Additionally, it's critical to ensure that your graphics drivers are current because outdated drivers might cause your computer to lag or crash. By routinely checking the manufacturer's website for the most recent graphics card drivers, you can prevent these kinds of issues. System resources can also be freed up by managing plugins and disabling unnecessary ones. To accomplish this, select File > Plug-in Manager and examine the list of loaded plugins.

Corruption in Catalogs

You might not be able to see your photos if your catalog becomes corrupted. This may occur when a disk problem occurs or when your machine abruptly shuts down. To lower this danger, you should frequently backup your catalog. You can restore the most recent backup by replacing the damaged catalog file with a copy from the backup in case something goes wrong. A built-in repair tool is another feature of Lightroom Classic. The software could ask you to repair any catalog damage it discovers. Usually, the issue can be resolved by following the instructions on the screen.

Problems with Imports

During the import procedure, users may encounter issues like photographs not appearing or the operation halting. These issues may arise from incorrect import settings or improper permissions in the target folder. If you wish to preserve the images in their current location, make sure the "Add" option is selected during import to ensure a seamless import. Additionally, confirm that Lightroom has the appropriate rights to write to the target folder and that it is entered correctly. On macOS, you may need to grant them access in System Preferences > Security & Privacy.

Develop Module Issues

Images may not change or sliders and modifications may not function properly in the Develop module. A GPU that isn't compatible with the game or incorrect settings could be the source of this behavior. Resetting preferences can correct unexpected behavior. To accomplish this, launch Lightroom while depressing Shift + Alt (Windows) or Shift + Option (macOS), and when prompted to reset preferences, select Yes. Try disabling GPU acceleration by selecting Edit > Preferences > Performance and unchecking Use Graphics Processor if the issues persist. This is due to the possibility that some GPUs may not be compatible with Lightroom, which could result in display issues.

Issues with Exporting

When you export images, the export process might not work at all or the files might not appear the same after editing. These problems are typically brought on by incorrect export settings or insufficient hard drive space. To ensure that the correct color space, file format, and quality parameters are selected, it is crucial to review the export settings. If these are incorrect, the outcomes could be unexpected. Additionally, it's critical to ensure that the target drive has sufficient disk space because insufficient space can cause the export operation to fail.

Problems Syncing with Adobe Cloud

You may view your photos from a variety of devices when you sync them with Adobe Cloud. But occasionally, things go wrong and the procedure takes a long time. The most common causes are network connectivity problems or sync problems. You must ensure that your internet connection is steady for sync to function properly. If the problems persist, checking the Sync Activity panel for errors or conflicts and resolving them by following the on-screen directions may be helpful.

Freezes and Crashes

It can be incredibly annoying when your computer freezes or crashes. Program incompatibilities or a poor startup could be the source of these issues. Lightroom Classic can be cleaned up and issues brought on by corrupted files can be resolved by reinstalling the program. Additionally, some programs could interfere with Lightroom's functionality. You can identify potential issues by briefly turning off background processes, such as security software.

Files or Folders Not Found

Images may occasionally display a "?" symbol, indicating the absence of files or directories. This typically occurs when external drives are turned off or when files are moved or altered outside of Lightroom. If you can't find the file you're looking for, right-click on it and select "Find Missing Folder" or "Find Missing Photo." Next, proceed to the location where the files were relocated. By making adjustments in Lightroom and maintaining a consistent file format, this issue can be avoided.

Resolving Cloud Storage and Syncing Issues

Adobe Lightroom Classic is a helpful application for photographers that allow you to edit and arrange images in a variety of ways. Nevertheless, users may occasionally encounter issues with cloud files and sync that prevent them from functioning. Your experience with the software can be much improved by being aware of these typical problems and how to resolve them. Getting Lightroom Classic and Adobe's cloud services to cooperate is one frequent issue. Users frequently complain that images don't sync between devices, that the process stalls, or that they receive error messages stating that the sync attempt was unsuccessful. Numerous factors, including catalog conflicts, outdated software versions, and network connection issues, could be the source of these problems. Since synchronization requires a stable network, you must ensure that your internet link is stable in order to resolve sync issues. Additionally, as updates frequently address known flaws and improve the program's functionality, you should confirm that you are using the most recent version of Lightroom Classic. It might also be useful to view specific errors or conflicts using Lightroom's Sync Activity window. To learn more about how the synchronization works and to see which files or collections aren't functioning properly, go to Preferences > Lightroom Sync and look at the Sync Activity section. Sometimes logging into Lightroom Web can help you learn more about sync issues and enable you to manually resolve them. Cloud storage issues, such as receiving notifications that the storage is full, experiencing difficulties sharing or syncing fresh images, or identifying discrepancies between locally saved and cloud-stored files, are another frequent problem. These issues typically arise when old files and sync faults consume up space or when the amount of data saved exceeds the cloud storage limit. To get the most out of your cloud storage, go over and arrange your files every day. Eliminating unnecessary files or backups can help you make space and prevent storage issues. Additionally, eliminate any sync errors that might be occupying space. You may optimize your cloud storage consumption by accessing Lightroom Web and removing any residual files or sync issues. Because files in the "Deleted" folder may still take up space in your cloud storage, be sure that this folder is also empty.

Additionally, users could notice that some images or collections don't update or that the syncing process is stalled, with the "sync" sign being on but no progress being made. If the sync data is corrupted or if earlier sync operations are terminated, this behavior may occur. Restarting the sync data could be helpful if the sharing procedure becomes stuck. Click on Rebuild Sync Data in Lightroom Classic while holding down the Alt (Windows) or Option (Mac) keys. Make sure you are in the Lightroom Sync > Preferences section. This action can restart the syncing process and resolve issues brought on by corrupted sync data. It might also be useful to identify and remove problematic images that are generating sync issues. Fixing the listed files and viewing the sync failures in the Sync Activity tab can be helpful. The inconsistency between local and cloud data is another issue. For instance, modifications and metadata might not sync correctly, or photos that are in the cloud and those that are displayed locally might not match. These discrepancies may arise when the sync fails or when the local and cloud copies of the files don't match. Due to these variations, manual resyncing of collections can be beneficial. One way to force a new sync and resolve issues is to take the problematic collection out of sync and then enable sync for that collection again. Additionally, confirm that the collections you wish to sync are appropriately labeled. To ensure that only the collections you wish to sync are involved in the process, click the "Sync" icon next to each collection. By adhering to common best practices, many issues with cloud files and sync can be avoided. You may prevent data loss in the event of sync problems by regularly backing up your Lightroom catalog and images. Monitoring your cloud storage usage will help you stay within your storage limit and prevent unexpected sync issues. You can take advantage of the latest features and eliminate issues that impact cloud storage and synchronization by keeping your software updated.

Getting in touch with Adobe Support and Troubleshooting Resources

Utilizing Adobe's testing tools and support resources will help you swiftly resolve issues with Adobe Lightroom Classic.

Reaching out to Adobe Help

Customers can seek assistance from Adobe in a number of ways:
- **Online Support Center:** The primary resource for assistance is Adobe's online support center, located at Adobe Support. You can use this to join group forums, learn lessons, and find solutions to common problems.
- **Direct Contact Options:** Adobe provides a variety of channels for you to contact them for individualized assistance. A customer service representative from the business is available by phone or live chat. Numerous contact details, including phone numbers and chat options, are available on Adobe's "Contact Us" website.
- **Community Forums:** Engaging with the Adobe Support Community can be beneficial. In the Lightroom Classic Community Forum, users may exchange experiences, ask questions, and receive assistance from other users as well as Adobe specialists.

Tools & Resources for Troubleshooting

Before contacting help, you might wish to try using Adobe's debugging tools:

- **Creative Cloud Diagnostic program:** This program examines your system for issues brought on by outdated drivers, broken hardware, or incompatible applications. Following the check, it provides you with a list of issues it discovered along with recommendations for solutions. This tool is located in the Creative Cloud app's "Help" section.
- **Lightroom Classic Debugging Guide:** Adobe offers a comprehensive guide to resolve typical Lightroom Classic problems, like as crashes, lag, and odd behaviors.
- **Graphics Processor (GPU) Troubleshooting:** If there are issues with the graphics processor, Lightroom Classic might not function as well. Adobe provides detailed information on how to resolve GPU and graphics driver issues.

Top Techniques for Effective Assistance

To ensure the success of your assistance:

- **Prepare Detailed Information:** Make sure to provide assistance with all relevant information when you contact, including error messages, recent system modifications, and the actions you took to cause the issue to recur. Evaluation and settlement proceed more swiftly as a result.
- **Keep Software Updates:** Since newer versions address a lot of issues, make sure your operating system and Adobe software are both up to date.
- **Frequent Backups:** You can prevent data loss while you're resolving issues by regularly backing up your Lightroom files and images.

You may efficiently handle and resolve issues that arise in Adobe Lightroom Classic by utilizing these tools and best practices, which will streamline and increase the productivity of your workflow.

Final Thoughts

More than just a photo editing program, Adobe Lightroom Classic 2025 is a comprehensive solution for photographers who wish to arrange, edit, and distribute their images in one location. We have covered every aspect of Lightroom Classic in this tutorial, from the fundamentals like importing your images and grouping them into folders and collections to more complex methods like applying masks, color grading, presets, and even personalizing your workspace. Lightroom Classic is great because it allows you complete control over your creative process without adding unnecessary complexity. Lightroom Classic is designed to meet your needs, whether you're a novice looking to add some color to your family photos or an experienced photographer working on a large project. It lets you eliminate undesirable items, improve colors, correct minor flaws, and even batch-edit hundreds of images at once without affecting the original. Lightroom Classic's ability to keep you organized is one of its greatest benefits. No more searching through files in vain for a picture. Catalogs, collections, ratings, keywords, and other features make it simple to find any picture, even if it was taken years ago.

It's also important to note that Lightroom Classic continues to advance annually. Better performance, more potent tools, and clever methods to speed up editing have all been incorporated in the 2025 version. However, Lightroom Classic will always be about helping you make your photographs look the way you want them to, regardless of how many new capabilities Adobe add. You now have all the information you need to utilize Lightroom Classic 2025 with confidence after finishing this instruction. Try out different tools and settings without fear. You will improve the more you practice. Additionally, keep in mind that editing is not about rigidly adhering to standards. Making each picture seem its best, adding your own touch, and using your images to convey a story are all important. Therefore, begin editing now. Lightroom Classic 2025 is prepared to assist you in realizing your vision, whether it's a straightforward sunset photo or a comprehensive professional photo session.